P9-AFP-590

# Does Literary Studies
# Have a Future?

# Does Literary Studies
# Have a Future?

❧

EUGENE GOODHEART

THE UNIVERSITY OF WISCONSIN PRESS

The University of Wisconsin Press
2537 Daniels Street
Madison, Wisconsin 53718

3 Henrietta Street
London WC2E 8LU, England

5       4       3       2       1

Printed in the United States of America

Library of Congress Cataloging-in-Publication Data

Goodheart, Eugene.
    Does literary studies have a future? / Eugene Goodheart.
    152 pp.        cm.
    Includes bibliographical references (p. 123) and index.
    ISBN 0-299-16650-3 (alk. paper)
    ISBN 0-299-16654-6 (pbk.: alk. paper)
    1. Criticism—United States—History—20th century.  2. Literature—
History and criticism—Theory, etc.  3. Literature—Study and teaching—
United States.  I. Title.
PN99.U5 G65  1999
801'.95'097309045—dc21        99-6270

For my mother in her nineties,
lover of books

# Contents

# Preface

Over one hundred years ago, when the Industrial Revolution was transforming the face, if not the soul, of England, John Henry Newman delivered a set of lectures on *The Idea of a University* in which he characterized the habit of mind formed by a liberal education as one of "freedom, equitableness, calmness, moderation and wisdom."[1] For the post-Enlightenment mind, the progress of knowledge assumes the increasing specialization of the disciplines, a counterpart to the division of labor in the industrial sphere. Newman anticipated the charge of being reactionary in advocating a reversal of the principle of the division of labor in defense of the liberal mind. For him, however, it was not a case of either/or. Without denying a place to the division of labor in the scholarly universe, he was properly fearful that the precious habit of mind formed by a liberal education would be lost in the triumph of the separate disciplines, and he was determined to champion its cause.

Specialization, particularly in the natural sciences, has accelerated since Newman's time, and the gulf between the sciences and the humanities is wider than ever. But that is not where the main threat to the liberal mind, now beset by its own internal conflicts, lies. If a wide gulf divides the natural sciences and the humanities, the disciplines of the humanities and the social sciences speak to each other. Assumptions from one discipline often migrate to other disciplines and produce an interdisciplinary mindset—for example, the assumption that tradition and innovation are opposing forces or that objectivity is an illusion. Tradition has come to be seen as the dead hand of the past, an obstacle to the acquiring of new knowledge. The case against the appeal to objectivity is more complicated. It reflects a view that each of us sees the world within the limitations of a particular point of view and that it is an imperializing presumption to claim that my or anyone else's view is objective truth. It follows then that the claim to objectivity often conceals the particular interest of a group (elite, class, race, etc.) that controls or has controlled the way we know the world. Conflicts arise about these assumptions within the disciplines, but not between them.

Against established ways of knowing, various identity groups have emerged (women, gays and lesbians, blacks, and other ethnic constituencies). Hitherto marginally represented in society at large and the academy, they have proposed new *theoretical* perspectives on matters of politics, social institutions, gender relationships, sexual preference, and the experience of literature. Theory itself has come to be identified with these new perspectives, and those who have resisted them have sometimes taken a position against theory. There are other occasions when the opposition to certain theoretical perspectives is an opposition to those perspectives and not to theory itself.

I cast a skeptical eye on the way the opposition between tradition and innovation, objectivism and perspectivism, aesthetics and ideology have been formulated. As I hope to show, the very terms in which the battles have been fought not only distort the issues at stake, but guarantee that nothing fruitful can emerge from these battles. The first chapter focuses on the work of "the cultural left," an infelicitous phrase that I employ *faute de mieux*. I devote the second chapter to the contribution the cultural right has made to our current predicament. The works of Dinesh D'Souza and Roger Kimball are among my examples. They relate devastating anecdotes about writing and behavior in the academy, but they are also unfair in their characterizations and judgments. They lack the disinterestedness and scholarly caution that they affirm. One reason may be that they write as outsiders, participants in conferences in which the academy often shows its worst side. They do not seem to know much about daily life in the classroom. Genre may also be part of the problem. Both Kimball and D'Souza display the journalist's talent for the critical sound bite, but not for extended argument. Indeed, rarely does a view of one of their adversaries warrant, in their eyes, serious treatment.

The third chapter takes up the formidable question of the canon and the classics that constitute it. I resist the idea that the justification of the traditional canon lies in its relevance to our immediate concerns. What I propose is an alternative view of the uncanniness of the classic. Rather than confirming our prejudices or even our interests, the classic may resist them. Difficult and strange, the classic succeeds if we discover the unfamiliar in ourselves: The moment of discovery produces the shock of recognition. The trouble with requiring the classic to be relevant to our immediate concerns is that it becomes a chameleon without integrity, a view, of course, congenial to the antiessentialist spirit of postmodernism. In the course of my discussion of the canon, I take up the ways in which critical theory has responded to the classic. I also devote a section to David Denby's interesting book about his "adventurous" return to the Great Books, as taught in Columbia College, after years as a film critic for *New York Magazine*. My discussion of Denby's book becomes an occasion for considering the teaching of literature and its effects on the minds and characters of students.

The canon is the site of high culture. Its most serious threat is popular culture. Watching television or browsing the internet are formidable diversions to the reading of serious literature. Popular culture has now become a significant subject in the curriculum. But it is not simply another subject. As taught in our colleges and universities, popular culture has as its agenda an attack on the claims of high culture. I spell out the affinities between this agenda and reader-centered theorizing about aesthetics. Current speculation about aesthetics tends to emphasize its illusory character, its dependence on the volatility and contingencies of consumer tastes (readers and spectators are consumers), its ephemerality. In short, it is speculation perfectly suited to the requirements of popular or mass culture.

I conclude with a chapter that bears the title of the book. I don't answer the question, "Does literary studies have a future?" with a yes or no. To do so would be a foolish venture into prophesy. What I try to do instead is to specify the conditions under which a fruitful academic study of literature might survive. Though the focus of the book will be on literary and cultural study as practiced in literature departments, it should be clear from my exposition that what I have to say has consequences for the humanities in general and even for the social sciences. Put differently, the practice of any discipline cannot be understood without placing it against the background of the cultural and academic assumptions it shares with other disciplines.

I know from reading reviews of my work and that of others that it will be characterized as moderate or centrist, neither fish nor fowl. I may be praised for being reasonable, but damned with the faintness of the praise for not having the edge of those at the extremes of the political and cultural spectrum. Someone once said that I "pull my punches." A friend speaks of me as "irenic." It is always risky to anticipate your critics. You don't want to be accused of defensiveness. But it is part of my argument that truth is not the exclusive possession of any particular perspective (not the same as saying that there are no objective truths) and that such an argument requires at once modesty as well as firmness in its expression.

In *The Education of Henry Adams,* Adams writes with condescension about a certain class of Englishmen which he encountered during his stay in London as private secretary to his father, the American minister to Great Britain: "These were trimmers, the political economist, the anti-slavery and doctrinaire class, the followers of Tocqueville, and of John Stuart Mill. As a class, they were timid—with good reason—and timidity, which is high wisdom in philosophy, sicklies the whole cast of thought in action."[2] In the chapter on eccentrics, Adams eccentrically characterizes the trimmer as "the most eccentric of all." I am not in the position to judge the behavior of the English followers of Mill and Tocqueville, but it is surely cynicism about the intellectual life to reduce the high wisdom of a Mill or Tocqueville (if Adams meant to include them as well) to timidity. Such a judgment does not correspond to the actual behavior of either of them in thought or action. It is one thing for a thinker or actor to compromise a principled commitment to reason and moderation and thereby become a trimmer. It is another thing to call reason and moderation ("the high wisdom of philosophy") trimming. Adams here manifests the debunking spirit, so characteristic of our cultural life today.

# Acknowledgments

Versions of chapters 1 and 2 appeared in and are reprinted by permission of *Daedalus,* Journal of the American Academy of Arts and Sciences, from the issue entitled "The American Academic Profession," Fall 1997, vol. 126, no. 4. A version of chapter 5 appeared in the *New England Review* (Winter 1998). I have also drawn passages from my articles "The Music of Henry James," *Partisan Review* (March 1997); "Literary Study Left and Right," *Transaction/Society* (January/February 1999); "The Demise of the Aesthetic in Literary Study," *Philosophy and Literature* (April 1997), copyright © 1997, The Johns Hopkins University Press; and "Arnold among the Neoconservatives," *Clio* (Summer 1996). I am grateful to Morris Dickstein and Millicent Bell for their helpful reading and enthusiastic support of my work. Peter Berger, Director of the Institute for the Study of Economic Culture at Boston University, offered me a grant from the Lynde and Harry Bradley Foundation to write this book. I am especially grateful to him and the Foundation for their support. Finally, I want to thank Andrea Most for her suggestions and assistance in preparing the manuscript and Melissa Feiden for her help in getting the manuscript in final shape.

# Does Literary Studies
# Have a Future?

# 1

⊚⊚

# Casualties of the Culture Wars

In *The Origins of Literary Study in America*, its editors, Gerald Graff and Michael Warner, remind us that controversy has always been a vital part of academic life. What we have today is not controversy, but war. The villains in this drama, Graff and Warner would have us believe, are traditional custodians of culture who foster a mystified "pastoral conception of the humanities as an 'overlay' of values which is to humanize the otherwise fallen realm of work and practical affairs . . . . It conveniently masks the fact that the humanities have always been a site of conflict and have never been immune to the incursions of industrialism."[1] In Graff and Warner's account, the traditionalists who hold this view become violent in their defense against the demystifiers. "What makes the current fulminations against the recent direction of literary studies so useless is that they are finally complaints about the presence of disagreement."[2] As the title of his recent book, *Beyond the Culture Wars*, tells us, Graff wants to get beyond warfare. Yet his own formulations reflect the pressures of combat. He favors the kind of debate that he says has characterized the profession of the humanities from its very beginnings and at the same time denies the validity of disagreement to those who conceive the profession differently. Are all the complaints against the demystifiers of the pastoral conception of the humanities "fulminations"? Could they not be described as disagreements? In Graff's scenario, to unmask the pastoral tradition is to disagree, to defend it is to fulminate. (I leave aside the question of whether "the pastoral conception of the humanities" is an accurate representation of the views of those who are the targets of demystification.)

3

"War" is something of a hyperbole with respect to events *within* the academy. The antitraditionalists have pretty much won the day. There are strong, discontented, academic voices, but they are a distinct and by no means united minority. I have in mind critics like Harold Bloom, Frank Kermode, and Robert Alter. The scholarly work in the new dispensation has become routine and, as we might expect, has lost some of the polemical edge that it had when in its insurgency. If there is war, it is being waged for the most part between those inside and those outside the academy. William Bennett, Dinesh D'Sousa, and Hilton Kramer are among the nonacademics who attack the academy and are themselves objects of attack.

Graff and Warner are right to describe the current situation as one in which adversaries do not respectfully disagree with each other. "Fulmination" is not wide of the mark in representing the tenor of many cultural encounters, but they are unfairly partisan in attributing the fulminations mainly to the conservative side. The fact is that cultural radicals as well as conservatives often substitute contempt for argument. Fruitful debate can occur in an atmosphere of mutual respect between adversaries, and this can be achieved only when the arguments on either side deserve respect. It is not that one or another of the opposing views that define the current conflict (examples: between universalists and multiculturalists, objectivists and antiobjectivists, defenders of the canon and critics of the canon) is intrinsically disreputable. There are admirable and less admirable expressions of each of the views. If the debate is to provide illumination, the antagonists must respond to the strongest possible formulations of their adversaries' views.

In an essay, "Preaching to the Converted," Graff chastizes the academic left for its arcane exclusionary rhetoric, its taking for granted of its own assumptions, the effect of which is to exclude "anyone [conservatives and even liberals] likely to say something about culture that might make academic leftists uncomfortable."[3] But one wonders whether this generous view of academic discourse is not a matter of tactics rather than an opening up to other points of view. Graff speaks of learning from the hostile media about "the organization of representations." The academic left has to represent itself in the public arena more effectively. "If we humanists refuse to learn something from these at-

tacks about the need to engage with those who disagree with us, our critics will continue to succeed in monopolizing the rhetoric of democracy
and in casting us as nattering nabobs of negativism."[4] "We humanists"
gives the game away. The critics of the academic left apparently don't
qualify as humanists; they are the opponents from whom one may learn
how to better represent one's views.

In *Beyond the Culture Wars*, Graff characterizes stereotypically the
older male professor's "defense of universality" as having "once put
generations of students to sleep." In his illustration, the old male professor turns out to be a female nonprofessor, Lynne Cheney, former head
of the National Endowment of the Humanities, whose use of "threadbare
phrases" like "what it means to be human" or "to know joy and find purpose nonetheless; to be capable of wisdom and folly" can "become interesting again" only when they are "challenged by the likes of a young
feminist professor."[5] Lynne Cheney's phrases may be threadbare. But in
identifying these phrases with an argument for universalism, one is
hardly doing justice to the possibilities of such an argument. Any serious quarrel with universalism must engage its most distinguished exponents: if not Plato, Descartes, and Kant, at least those in the intellectual
tradition they inspired. A benefit of taking on a strong adversary is that
your ideas may be challenged and strengthened in the process.

Another benefit is the discovery of the weaknesses and limitations
of your own view. The encounter with a strong adversary becomes an exercise in self-criticism. In his essay on Coleridge, John Stuart Mill, the
liberal, examines conservative social and political thought not to affirm
the superiority of liberalism, but to learn what conservatism in its most
impressive formulation can teach liberals. The impulse in Mill to do so
derived from his perception of a radical deficiency in the mindset of his
mentor. Bentham "failed in deriving light from other minds."[6] During his
mental crisis, Mill became painfully aware of the limitations and inadequacies of his own understanding as well as of his emotional constitution. From this discovery, he concluded that self-criticism should be the
basis for intellectual formation. Learning becomes a struggle with oneself, a willingness to think against oneself.

Mill's mental crisis did not result in a conversion experience. It produced a discovery about the nature of the truth that expanded and

fortified his liberalism. Truth, he came to see, was many-sided, and no single mind possessed a monopoly of it. If he had converted to the romantic–conservative outlook of Carlyle or Coleridge or Burke, he would have traded one certainty for another. The view that truth is not to be found at a single site and is dispersed throughout society is the epistemological basis of democracy. We tolerate the views of others not because of an imperative to be kind and tolerant, but because of what we may learn from those views. The many-sidedness of truth is not a provisional belief to be surrendered when the mind achieves absolute truth. Absolute truth, a monolithic creature, is an impossibility. Like the messiah, it may be desired, but its arrival should be dreaded, for it is a tyrant. In practice, most liberals think of conservatives as being beyond the pale and vice versa. As notional believers in democracy, they tolerate the others' existence, but they don't credit their adversaries as being in possession of a truth or having a real claim to be heard and respected.

The very idea of a culture war is inimical to a model of education as self-criticism (for that is what Mill's essays on Bentham and Coleridge propose). A warrior acquires weapons to achieve victory. In the cultural sphere, the weapons of choice are words and ideas. The cultural warrior attends to the words and ideas of his adversaries not to learn from them, but to discover those weaknesses that he can then exploit to his own advantage. Attack and defense become the dominant cultural style. The very formulation of the issues that divide adversaries guarantees that they will not listen to each other. Even Graff, who can be a generous and fair expositor of ideas, effectively disenfranchises the side with which he is not sympathetic by the way he states its basic terms.

Consider, for example, his conception of the opposing forces in the academy. On one side is a fixed tradition, on the other innovation and novelty. "The modern university has from the very beginning rested on a deeply contradictory mission. The university is expected to preserve, to transmit and honor our traditions, yet at the same time it is supposed to produce new knowledge."[7] And elsewhere Graff and his collaborator Michael Warner speak of "the authority of tradition [as] being inherited rather than assembled through debate, its defining values as axiomatic. Historically, professional literary criticism has found itself between the opposing needs of constructing debatable hypotheses, on the one hand,

and preserving a normative heritage, on the other."[8] The view that there is an inherent opposition between tradition and new knowledge (hence making the mission of the academy contradictory) rests on the assumption that tradition is a fixed or petrified corpus and cannot be the source of new ideas.

In a recent article in the widely circulated magazine *Civilization*, David Damrosch makes a similar distinction between "the preservation and transmission of culture" and "the production of knowledge," which until recently has corresponded to a distinction between the humanities and the sciences. Preservation and transmission are uncritically conflated, so that transmission becomes a mere repetition of the past rather than what it is, a mediation of the past in the new circumstances of the present. Every mediation effects a change by giving the cultural past a new look, if it doesn't actually transform it. In which case, the distinction between the transmission of culture and the production of knowledge collapses. Damrosch associates the production of knowledge with a "skeptical, analytic mode."[9] It is not clear how a respectful and even reverent interpretation of a text, for example, that adds to other interpretations is to be distinguished from a skeptical or analytic approach in terms of the production of knowledge. What is there in skepticism that is intrinsically the source of new knowledge? One can imagine a skepticism about new approaches that obstructs the advancement of knowledge.

Even Alan Wolfe, an astute critic of stereotypes in current cultural discourse, embraces the stereotypical disparagement of tradition. "Those who defend tradition, believe in authority and obedience, and assign a relatively low priority to reason and argumentation are not going to find social criticism to their liking." And yet, in a sentence that immediately follows, the social critics who affirm reason and argumentation are understood to have their own tradition. "In this broad sense, social criticism, a product of Enlightenment values, belongs to the liberal tradition."[10] Tradition is the inescapable possession of anyone who thinks and acts.

There are, of course, breaks from tradition, but they are the work of remarkable intellects, who in turn inaugurate traditions. Innovation (i.e., genuine and significant innovation) from scholars, intellectuals, and artists does not arise as a matter of course. Most scholars work in an established tradition, whether new or old. And even the tablet breakers, the inaugurators of new ideas, do not come ex nihilo from a tradition-free space. At this late date in the history of art and ideas, it is hard not to find anticipations of the new in the old. Foucault is foreshadowed in Nietzsche, Derrida in Nietzsche and Heidegger, and Freud in Romanticism. This is remarked not to disparage innovation but rather to specify its conditions.

The opposition between tradition and innovation is imported from the sciences, where ignorance of the achievements of the past does not constitute an obstacle to scientific discovery. The model of the sciences does not apply to the humanities where discoveries are of a different order and where indeed discovery in the sense of "the production of new knowledge" may not be an apt characterization of humanistic study. As David Bromwich remarks, "scholarly discovery in the humanities does now and then produce new knowledge. That is only one of the interesting things it does. It may also (by a fresh arrangement of facts) help to create the intuitions of a whole generation. And it may (by a stroke of interpretative acuteness) serve as a stimulus to further discovery or as an incitement to thinking."[11] It is something of an irony or paradox that the model of science should be imported into the humanities at a time when the scientific ideal of objective knowledge has become the object of a radically skeptical mistrust in the humanities.

Tradition entails both change and continuity. Within it, arguments occur about its meaning, new conceptions of its significance arise. Neither the Marxist nor the Freudian tradition is a fixed legacy of the figure who inspired it. T. S. Eliot, the most conservative of modernists, understood the relationship between tradition and the individual talent as a dialectic between change and continuity. Even "making it new" has already a tradition as Harold Rosenberg pointed out in an essay in which he coined the phrase "the tradition of the new." Tradition, as conceived by Graff and Damrosch, resembles the view attributed to William Bennett by Peter Brooks: "an inherited body of knowledge—itself embodying certain transcendent 'values'—which has assumed fixed form and should be preserved and transmitted, by teachers and scholars, with fidelity and reverence." Brooks, it seems to me, is much closer to the reality of tradition when he speaks of it as "an historical culture formation, based on readings, interpretations, discriminations performed by people and cultural institutions in historical time." The view of tradition as fixed "represses the fact that traditions not only shape individual interpretations but are themselves the product of interpretation."[12] (In Harold Bloom's more radical view, tradition is a conflict between past and present, a struggle between inheritance and new departures. "Tradition is not only a handing-down, a process of benign transmission; it is also a conflict between past genius and present aspiration, in which the prize is literary survival or canonical inclusion."[13]) If both sides were understood to have different stakes in tradition, the debate would take on a quite different cast. The cultural radical might find his own view enriched by attending to his tradition. The conservative would be compelled to affirm what is alive in his sense of tradition. Nothing new and worthwhile can be produced without having its source in some tradition. As Tzvetan Todorov puts it, "the goal of a humanist, liberal education, is to form minds that are simultaneously tolerant and critical. The method employed to attain this goal is the mastery of a particular tradition."[14]

There is no single tradition; traditions are multiple and often in disagreement with one another. Consider, for example, Allan Bloom's extremely controversial understanding of tradition in *The Closing of the American Mind*. One need not be an antitraditionalist to quarrel with it, as I do. For Bloom, the Greek classics (in particular, Plato) and democracy are opposed. His argument in behalf of the classics is directed less against democracy than it is against the academy's subservience to it and in particular its populist American version. The distinction is important because, like Tocqueville, he accepts the political reality of democracy as irreversible, though with less grace. Modern democracy has its origins in the Enlightenment. One of Bloom's main objections to the Enlightenment is that it married philosophy and politics, or put differently, it conceived the role of philosophy as a transforming agent of society and the state. Bloom is a follower of Socrates, who believes in a tension between philosophy and politics. It is the academy ideally that should enact the Socratic role of critic, but it has failed to do so. Instead it mimics all the vices of democracy.[15]

It is hardly surprising that Bloom would be denounced by the cultural left and shunned by those of liberal disposition. (I must confess to having avoided *The Closing of the American Mind* for the longest time.

When I read it, I found myself intrigued, though unconvinced by Bloom's "idiosyncratic" [his word] account of the intellectual history of the West.) There is no scandal in the view that Socrates has something to teach and that the postmodern university commits a dereliction of duty in not taking the classics seriously. The trouble with Bloom (even for many "traditionalists") is that for him the process of education is a one-way street. All the wisdom of the world is contained in the classics. (If Shakespeare is the canon for Harold, Plato is it for Allan.) Modern society, for Bloom, is a nihilism—without values or with the wrong values. Much of the book is given over to a diagnosis of the ills of American democracy (it is not always clear whether Bloom is describing modern America or the modern world). We are given nothing of the kind of understanding that the aristocrat Alexis de Tocqueville displays of why democracy with its egalitarian ethos is an irreversible process. We get no sense in Bloom's book of the appeal of democracy. Bloom assumes, but does not demonstrate, Socrates's unparalleled wisdom. In his view of the world and the academy, modernity and democracy have nothing to teach—except perhaps the lessons of nihilism. It should then not come as a surprise for Bloom that Celine rather than Mann or Camus is the great modern writer, for he reveals with unequaled honesty the corruption and vacuity of the age. Bloom's modernity is Eliot's waste land.

Democracy versus aristocracy is an ahistorical polarization of ideas, attitudes, and realities. According to the stereotype, democracy stands for equality and aristocracy for liberty. But there are democratic liberties or freedoms that one could not experience in an aristocratically based society, and equality in a democracy does not preclude merit-based distinctions. Jefferson, as we know, envisioned a meritocratic democracy: equality of opportunity, but not of result. Nothing of these distinctions enters Bloom's discourse. No doubt a brilliant teacher, Bloom could teach the classics interestingly, even persuasively, from his "idiosyncratic" point of view, but his particular take on the classics can hardly become a model for the academy as a whole. (The appeal of Bloom's book [it sold over a million copies] was, of course, not based on his view of intellectual history, but rather on his jeremiad-like musings about pop culture, for instance, rock music. It addressed a middle-class mood of discontent with life in America.)

Allan Bloom's argument proves, if proof is needed, that the valuing of tradition does not follow a prescribed pattern which all traditionalists follow. It is not simply that there are differences and disagreements about the tradition; tradition itself is a scene or series of scenes of quarrels among the classics. Bloom, the disciple of Socrates and Plato, admires Nietzsche's intellectual power, while rejecting his critique of Socrates and the Socratic tradition. Indeed, Nietzsche and Locke, among others, are great antagonists in Bloom's view of the tradition. In her review of Bloom's book, the classicist and philosopher Martha Nussbaum takes Bloom to task not for his "traditionalism," but rather for his conception of tradition, particularly the one that originates with Socrates. Nussbaum's Socrates is a questioning and self-questioning spirit who serves to strengthen democratic culture; Bloom's is a critic of democracy.[16] My purpose here is not to decide between the two views, but rather to make the rather evident point that tradition itself has always been the scene of contestation, that virtually no view, even the most strident antitraditionalist view, rises ex nihilo. This argument has been made about the literary tradition by the other Bloom (Harold), who understands the very drive to originality in the great poets as an anxious but necessarily futile attempt to escape its grip (i.e., the achievement of the great predecessor poets). The attempt does produce something new and compelling, but it continues to bear the marks and contain the echoes of the tradition.

Can opposing views of tradition be adjudicated or does the quarrel between them become an insurmountable impasse? Sometimes differences between reasonable antagonists can be resolved by an appeal to evidence. But more often than not what is involved are opposing or different takes on the evidence. But even between irreconcilable antagonists, there is usually an agreement which makes a common scholarly and intellectual enterprise possible. There are two kinds of valuing of writers, thinkers, and artists in the tradition: intellectual and imaginative power and the right deployment of that power, so it is possible for Bloom and Nussbaum to be in agreement about Socrates as a classic, but to disagree in their deployment of him in their arguments. One might regard a writer or thinker as an adversary, as Bloom views Nietzsche or as T. S. Eliot at one time viewed Milton, and yet acknowledge his place and power in the tradition. It is, of course, possible to reject a whole tradition, that of high culture, for instance, in the name of something else (popular culture), but even such gestures have their antecedents in a tradition.

"Tradition" is not the only misunderstood term in the culture wars. Just as tradition has been opposed to innovation, objectivity has been set against perspectivism with the first term representing a conservative and the second term a radical or liberal view. Objectivists are universalists who affirm a common culture, perspectivists multiculturalists who champion diversity. A stranger to the conflicts might find it odd that the cultural left has identified itself with an antiuniversalist view. It was after all one of the founders of modern conservatism, the reactionary Joseph De-Maistre, who said: "There is no such thing as *man* in the world. I have seen, during my life, Frenchmen, Italians, Russians, etc. But as far as *man* is concerned, I declare I have never in my life met him; if he exists, he is unknown to me."[17] Ideas of objectivity, universality, and commonality, the legacy of Enlightenment progressivism, have by an irony of history become objects of leftist suspicion. They are seen as ideological masks to justify the particular interests of the dominant culture. And there is an additional irony in the fact that what counts as innovation in the binary opposition between tradition and innovation is an identity politics that tries to recover the ethnic experiences of the past. It is no objection to the efforts of African Americans, Hispanics, Jews, Italians, and so on to want to retrieve what is valuable in their traditions. What it shows however is the illusoriness of the opposition between tradition and innovation.

Antiuniversalism, antiobjectivism, antiessentialism are now the shibboleths of a movement, requiring no thought. "As with most colleagues I respect," writes a distinguished member of the profession, "my antis are impeccable: I am antifoundationalist, anti-essentialist, anti-universalist, and I do not believe in the possibility of that view from nowhere that gets one beyond contingency."[18] This is an unreflective declaration of party affiliation. It is also a misconception of the adversary view. Foundationalism is not a matter of getting somewhere from nowhere. On the contrary, it is the antifoundationalist who begins from nowhere. Apparently respect for colleagues depends not on their quality of mind, but rather on their position in the political–cultural spectrum. There is even an implication of disrespect for thinkers of the caliber of Descartes, Kant, and Chomsky. It should be noted that the antiuniversalist view has not gone un-challenged on the left. In his recent book, *The Twilight of Common Dreams: Why America Is Wracked by Culture Wars*, Todd Gitlin points out the disastrous political and social consequences of a militant par-ticularist identity politics.

For the Left as for the rest of America, the question is not whether to recognize the multiplicity of American groups, the variety of American communities, the disparity of American experiences. Those exist as long as people think they exist. The question is one of proportion. What is a Left without a commons, even a hypothetical one? If there is no people, but only peoples, there is no Left.[19]

I would emend the last sentence to say: There is no humanity. What Gitlin doesn't say, but may be implied by his criticism, is that academic identity politics may not be a politics in any effective sense. Whatever resonance it has is within the academy or in the mockery by those out-side the academy. I know of serious liberals and even radicals in the labor movement and other political organizations who are simply be-mused by what passes for politics in the academic left.

The disreputable status of objectivity, as it plays itself out in the cur-rent debates, is, in my view, a result of the tendentious manner in which the term is understood. Even such a prized work as Peter Novick's *That Noble Dream: The "Objectivity Question" and the American Historical Profession* formulates "the question" in such a way that it becomes hard to understand how a sophisticated intellectual can subscribe to the ob-jectivist view. Here is Novick's sympathetic description of the anti-objectivist challenge in the 1960s:

In one field after another distinctions between fact and value and between the-ory and observation were called into question. For many, postures of disinter-estedness and neutrality increasingly appeared as outmoded and illusory. It ceased to be axiomatic that the scholar's or scientist's task was to represent ac-curately what was "out there." Most crucially, and across the board, the notion of a determinate and unitary truth about the physical or social world, ap-proachable if not ultimately reachable, came to be seen by a growing number of scholars as a chimera.[20]

Novick writes as a historian, and his account accurately reflects dis-tinctions made by others, but he accepts them uncritically. Value-laden statements allow for objectivity. A person is not prevented from objectively pursuing injustice by his passion for justice. Disinterestedness in a judge is a means of rising above prejudice to discover the truth and administer justice. And one may believe in the possibility of objectivity without believing in "the notion of a determinate and unitary truth," just as one can be a perspectivist and hold the view that statements can be judged objectively from a particular point of view as true or false. (Perspectivism and objectivism are not necessarily opposed, as Novick suggests they are elsewhere in his book.)[21] Objectivity has unfortunately become the sign for a cluster of ideas (absolute or unitary truth, value-neutral fact, perspective-free observation) that is not entailed in the idea of objectivity.

The fact is that objectivity or the appeal to it is inescapable in any forum in which ideas are argued and debated.[22] If that were not the case, the intellectual enterprise would be impossible. Since disagreements could never be overcome by an appeal to fact or reason, why would one bother to engage in reasoned debate? (Novick himself implicitly claims objectivity for himself when in his introduction he speaks of his "even-handedness" and "detachment," as he has to, if he means to be persuasive.[23]) The antiobjectivist view begins with the truth that objectivity is difficult to attain; it leaps illicitly to the conclusion that it is an impossible and undesirable ideal. Undesirable because objectivity is confused with the authoritarian implications of absolute truth. This is a paradoxical conclusion in light of the fact that the suppression of the search for objective truth is a feature of tyranny. The rulers of Oceania in George Orwell's *1984* perpetuate their rule by denying potential rebels and dissidents access to the facts of both the past and the present that would expose the lies and corruption of the rulers. The truth of Orwell's insight into the connection between objective knowledge and freedom is, of course, confirmed not only by the most egregious examples (Nazi Germany and the Soviet Union), but by tyrannies everywhere. One can only speculate about the insensitivity of postmodern theory, the theory of the cultural left, to this fact. Could it be that the very freedom of our society makes it possible for it to be taken for granted and for a condition of that freedom to be disparaged?

Objectivity assumes that reason has a certain autonomy, that it is not interest-driven in the narrow sense of interest. Let us, however, suppose the contrary—that reason is not an autonomous force, that it always expresses desires and interests. What are the desires and interests of the rational or reasonable person? The fear that without rational criteria for judgments, force will become the "court" of appeal. The fear, perhaps out of a sense of weakness, that the charismatic power of voice or the strength of body will resolve issues of contention.

I am sure that Richard Rorty, the most forceful contemporary philosopher of the antiobjectivist view, would quarrel with my account of it. As a passionate advocate of solidarity, he appreciates the need for common understandings and would substitute intersubjectivity for objectivity. "[W]e deny that the search for objective truth is a search for correspondence to reality, and urge that it be seen instead as a search for the widest possible intersubjective agreement."[24] And how would this agreement be achieved without having recourse to objective appeals to reality when necessary? The subject of the essay from which I have just quoted is academic freedom and its philosophical suppositions. "Philosophers on my side of the argument think that if we stop trying to give epistemological justifications, and instead give sociopolitical justifications, we shall be both more honest and more clearheaded. We think that disinterested, objective inquiry would not only survive the adoption of our philosophical views but survive in a desirably purified form."[25]

I am not sure what it means to give "sociopolitical justifications," apart from displaying your party credentials to the like-minded and demonstrating how your words and actions serve a particular cause. How this would serve disinterested, objective inquiry is not at all clear. Given Rorty's view that objectivity is an illusion, it seems intellectually irresponsible to appropriate its language for his view and then to assert that he has purified objectivism, when in fact he has undermined it. (Rorty's idea of social–political justification is a benign version of Foucault's idea of knowledge and power as seamlessly connected. Unlike Rorty, Foucault dispenses with the idea of disinterestedness altogether.)

There is a potential for intolerance in both objectivist and relativist outlooks, in those who are universalists and those who are particularists. Objectivism may mask and impose a subjective "truth" on others; relativists may refuse to listen to beliefs that are not their own. But objectivity in theory and often in practice proposes a standard of adjudication outside the quarreling parties.

I am less concerned to score points against Rorty than to show how difficult, if not impossible, it is for even the most persuasive of anti-objectivists to escape the claim of objectivism. Instead of confronting the claim, they avoid or displace it from the question of how we know the world to political struggle. Here is Evelyn Fox Keller agreeing with Rorty:

> Rorty is right: invocations of epistemology are beside the point; indeed, they are simultaneously misleading and counterproductive. The crisis we face today is real enough, but it has far less to do with arguments about the locus or status of ontological Truth than it has to do with current social, political, and economic realities. Terms like "objectivity" and "PC" have become weapons in the social, political and economic struggles in which we are all embedded.[26]

Though Keller wants to get beyond the culture wars, her very formulation of the issues is a contribution to the combat. By capitalizing "Truth," she illicitly identifies the objectivist conceptions with absolutist views of truth. By enclosing "objectivity" and "PC" in quotation marks, she makes clear who the culprits are. There is no acknowledgment in the passage that the words enclosed in quotation marks may be weapons on both sides. She does acknowledge that she is embedded in the struggles, but gives little indication about what part she plays.

Postmodernism is the covering name given to identity politics (which is the politics of race, gender, sexual preference, and class). Perspectivism (that is to say, antiobjectivist, antiuniversalist theory) provides its epistemological basis. But it claims to be more than a particular theory. Having inherited the authority of theory from poststructuralism (in particular, deconstruction), postmodernist advocates construe all attacks on their cultural theory as attacks on theory itself. Here again we have a case of a tendentious formulation of the issue.

But first we need to acknowledge the truth in the charge. Some critics do write from a bias against theory, a bias that goes as far back as Matthew Arnold, who mistrusted all systematic thinking in the humanities and emphasized the importance of flexibility and suppleness in the exercise of the critical intelligence. For T. S. Eliot, the one thing needful was intelligence, and F. R. Leavis toward the end of a long career decidedly hostile to theoretical reflection about literature finally found what might be called an antitheoretical theory congenial to his own views. The work of Michael Polanyi, mediated through Marjorie Grene, gave Leavis what he wanted, a conception of knowledge (Polanyi called it "tacit") that allowed for the play of intuition in criticism.

The current heirs of Arnold, Eliot, and Leavis tend to be British critics like Denis Donoghue and Christopher Ricks, who advocate the cultivation of theory-free reading zones in which the local pleasures and meanings of the text become manifest.[27] But in our theoretical age, even they cannot avoid a confrontation with theory. As the theorists legitimately claim, no one can perform, whether consciously or not, an intellectual task without assumptions and implications that have a theoretical bearing. Even Leavis felt obliged to reflect about what he was doing as a critic. Which of course does not mean that critics are obliged to subscribe to a theory or, as one says nowadays, "theorize" the practical work that they do. They may legitimately want to resist a theoretical formulation of their work to preserve a sense of freedom, flexibility, and complexity. A *conscious* employment of theory can be stultifying. What distinguishes an untheoretical criticism is the personal voice of the critic, assuming of course that the critic has a personality. Postmodern theory, disbelieving in the integrity of the subject (i.e., the self), has effectively exorcized the personal voice. The postmodern critic enters a discourse in which his prose becomes stylistically indistinguishable from other practitioners of the discourse. It is the discourse, not the person, that writes.

Not all critics of current theory are hostile to theory per se. What some find distressing is the lack of sophistication and rigor in the theorizing and an obscurantist idiom that often conceals it. Writing apropos of the Sokal affair (in which a physicist at New York University, Alan Sokal, submitted an article on science parodying the idiom of postmodern theory to the postmodern journal, *Social Text*, which its editors took seriously enough to publish), the philosophers Paul Boghosian and Thomas Nagel deplore "the sloppy and naive quality of what passes for philosophical argument and . . . the central role that such argument has been meant to play."[28] Apparently it is enough for a writer to use the jargon of a particular ideological discourse fluently to impress the community of discoursers that something is being said—or at least to prevent them from seeing through the nonsense. The Sokal affair also exposed an embarrassing bad faith in the postmodern editors of *Social Text*, who placed the responsibility of their failure to tell the difference between a genuine work of scholarship and a parody of it on Sokal for producing the hoax. (The failure of the editors of *Social Text* is not that they failed to see the hoax. Without scientific knowledge, they could not be expected to pass judgment. Their failure was in not consulting with scientific authorities. Perhaps they suspected that established scientific authority was so opposed to postmodernism that the essay would not get a fair hearing from a scientist. But if no respected scientist could be found to endorse the essay, wouldn't that be sufficient reason to doubt its validity?) The real issue for philosophical critics like Boghosian and Nagel is not whether "doing theory" is worthwhile, but the value of what passes for theory. For them the question is not whether to theorize or not to theorize, but the character and quality of the theory.

The culture wars have been largely waged within the provinces of the humanities and, to a lesser extent, the social sciences—over different conceptions of the disciplines. The problem of miscomprehension between science and the humanities, addressed decades ago by C. P. Snow in his little book, *The Two Cultures,* has undergone a significant development. Snow argued that humanists were woefully ignorant of and indifferent to scientific knowledge. Postmodern theorists, as if in belated response to Snow, have renewed the science–humanities conflict by putting in question fundamental tenets of scientific knowledge—the possibility of objective knowledge and its progressive character. On the one hand, "science studies" under postmodern sponsorship tries to undermine what the postmoderns consider the complacency of the scientific community about the objective and progressive character of scientific knowledge. On the other hand, scientists and philosophers of science have been provoked both by antiobjectivist arguments and by the crudity of their formulation. Often obscurantist, postmodern rhetoric asserts the impossibility of objective truth (lower- as well as uppercase) without the fine-grained engagement with the issues that mark the work of professional philosophers trained in the analytic school. Postmodernist theories have been largely unchallenged, because rigor in theorizing is not sufficiently cultivated within the humanities, so it always is a salutary event when those who have knowledge about theory making respond to the theories.

The effect of misleading and tendentious formulations of the issues is to disenfranchise one side or another from the debate by making it impossible to say certain things that should be said. This is particularly the case in matters that are more directly political than epistemological. For instance, ideology critics have a field day exposing colonialist motives and motifs in texts and institutions. Those who wish to defend these texts and institutions are at a distinct disadvantage. Who would want to defend a demystified imperialism? The usual tack is to deflect the charge of imperialism by denying its presence or relevance or minimizing its significance. What is off-limits is any effort to show the benefits of colonialism. I recall a meeting with a Marxist-leaning Indian foreign exchange professor in which he expressed contempt for Western scholars of what is called subaltern studies, who regularly denounce imperialism and its legacy in India and elsewhere without knowing the actual facts on the ground. It was the Brahmins, not the English colonialists, who maintained the caste system. It was the English colonizers who created educational opportunities for the Untouchables. According to the Indian professor, the departure of the English did not improve the lot of the Untouchables or, for that matter, those on the lower rungs of the caste system. On the contrary, their conditions have worsened. Truth is not served in denying the facts; nor is imperialism served in expressing them.

How did the current situation arise? The story has been told again and again of 1960s radicals who established themselves in the academy in the 1970s and 1980s and transformed their activism into theories of interpretation. Having lost the political battles in the early 1970s (the general society and its politics grew increasingly conservative), they transferred their energies to the academic arena. Texts in the humanities became the terrain on which political battles were to be fought. Literary works were now read not for their artfulness or wisdom but for their ideological motives. But that is not the whole story.

Lynn Hunt has tried to explain how these new theories of interpretation have maintained their authority once having achieved it. She presents statistics to show the remarkable increase in multiethnic and female students in an era of declining resources and concludes that "scholars in the humanities must meet the demographic and cultural challenge."[29] She is right, I think, in describing what has been felt to be the new scholarly imperative. There is a question, however, about what the interests of students are and how they should be responded to. It is not at all clear that a change in student demographics means that students entering the university necessarily expect to be educated in identity politics. Some do and others do not. My own experience is that boredom or resistance to any subject matter is no respector of racial or ethnic or gender difference. It may of course have to do with the quality of teaching. Or it may be a reflection of the influences of popular culture. The question for which there is no simple answer is: How should universities take account of student expectations and resistances? One would want to distinguish between expectations and resistances that expose weaknesses in the curriculum and those that need to be resisted and overcome because they reflect failures in the students.

The opposition to change in the academy has proved to be less formidable than the conservative force of society in general and its political structures. The intellectual and moral passion that had created the New Criticism, for example, was spent. Scholars of English literature were running out of subjects. Structuralism, deconstruction, ideology critique focusing on race, gender, and class, and the study of popular culture generated a new energy and excitement in the academy. It encountered little opposition, because the scholarly establishment lacked the conviction of the insurgents. What I am describing did not occur everywhere in the academy. I suspect that many institutions of higher learning in the country have not experienced an academic transformation, and that there are still places where the older traditions of teaching prevail. (Francis Oakley makes a case for skepticism about "the direct transfer of the scholarly or critical preoccupations of the more avant garde among those doing the publishing into their own undergraduate teaching.")[30] But the transformation did take place in the leading institutions which have a disproportionate influence not only on academic, but also on the cultural life generally. Occurrences at Yale or Hopkins or Duke capture the attention of the mass media and shape the perceptions of a large section of the population of what is occurring in the academy.

What explains intellectual intolerance inside and outside the academy is the politicization of academic discourse. If politics occupies the entire space of discourse, you are no longer required to persuade others of the rightness of your views by appealing to reason (i.e., logic and evidence). Indeed, you cannot hope to persuade the other side, because of the assumption that what determines the opposing view are interests, hidden or open, that are not amenable to reason. Intellectual exchange becomes disdainful rhetorical encounters in which each side affirms itself without the prospect of common agreement. Differences between the like-minded can be adjudicated (i.e., among cultural conservatives or among cultural radicals), but between opposing sides, reasonable exchange is very difficult, if not impossible, precisely because "socio–political" rather than "epistemological justification" (Rorty's phrases) is the order of the day. Academic intellectuals are no longer required to justify knowledge, they need only tell us what they believe.

## II

In my own discipline of literary studies, ideology critique rules the roost. It is a species of the hermeneutics of suspicion and one of the sources of the culture war. There is nothing more aggressive than the effort to demystify the supposed illusions of others. As I have written previously, "real debate or dialogue becomes impossible, because the ground between demystifier and antagonist is not the problematic nature of truth [or an uncertainty about where the truth lies], but the difference between truth and illusion. The person who claims to know the truth and is *certain* that others with an opposing view are the captives of illusion is a potential despot."[31] Here is a paradox: Those who possess this certainty about the illusions of others usually call themselves antifoundationalists, antiessentialists, and antiuniversalists. And they are suspicious of all claims to objectivity. So where does their certainty about the mystifications of others come from? Apparently from a conviction about the moral superiority of their side in the cultural and political struggles. If mystification conceals motives of domination, then the moral task of criticism is to unmask these motives.

Unlike perspectivists who tend toward skepticism about all claims to objectivity, ideology critics equivocate on the question of objectivity. They would claim it for their demystifications, but at the same time share with perspectivists a sensitivity to the partiality and self-interestedness of all points of view. Ideology critique can be a valuable activity if it knows its limits, discriminating between what requires and what does not require demystification. In contemporary practice in the academy, it has become an imperial obsession with disastrous consequences.

One casualty of this obsession in literary study is the virtual disappearance of the practice of aesthetic criticism. A number of years ago at an Modern Language Association convention I was on a search committee interviewing candidates for a position in Victorian literature in our department. One of the candidates had done a dissertation on Christina Rossetti in which "Goblin Market" played a prominent role. As I recall, the candidate was putting forth a New Historicist or feminist argument about the poem, when one of my colleagues on the committee interrupted her with the question: "But is it a good poem?" The question took me by surprise, for I didn't remember such a question having been asked of students in years. It dumbfounded the candidate. She had apparently never considered the question. The poem was there as an occasion for . . . I was about to write interpretation or analysis, but it would be more accurate to say: a placement in a particular discourse—historicist, feminist, deconstructionist, ideological. The candidate's fluency about the poem came to a halt. She spluttered a few phrases about the power of the poem. She was unprepared to answer the question, having never been asked or taught to ask it by her teachers of any poem or novel or play that she had read.

We may not have been fair in our judgment of her. If we had been consistent and asked the same question of all the candidates, I do not think we would have met with greater success. Our candidate's disability was, indeed still is, built into the profession of literary studies at the present time. The distinction Jane Gallop makes between the New Criticism and poststructuralism is symptomatic of the current state of affairs: "When New Criticism held sway in the literary academy, the reigning values were aesthetic. By the mid-1980s the dominant discourse in the literary academy is poststructuralist and the reigning values are theoretical. Where once the academic feminist looked to Emily Dickinson, now she pins her hopes on Julia Kristeva."[32] The aesthetic can no longer achieve the dignity of theory; it has become its antonym. That aesthetic judgment is not one of the current professional practices is clear not only from its absence in the content of literary study but from the styles of the discoursers. No longer written in a vernacular style, criticism has become a species of sociological prose once held in contempt by literary scholars—ponderous, abstract, obscure, ungainly, jargonish. There are practitioners of New Historicism, ideology critique, and deconstruction who write well, but who seem to regard their own gifts of expression as incidental, and are not in the least discomfited by the bad writing of others.

Style is not an incidental matter. Orwell made a compelling case for its political and moral significance. In his classic essay "Politics and the English Language," he preached the virtues of plain speech, the transparent and elegant style as a mark of self-honesty. (Transparency makes it difficult to conceal your ideas from yourself.) In *Writing Degree Zero* and subsequent writings, Roland Barthes deconstructed, so to speak, the Enlightenment myth of transparency as a guarantor of honesty and truth. Reality was not as perspicuous to "natural" plain writing as the Enlightenment believed. Barthes's own style (rich, inventive, personal, alternately perspicuous and obscure) is that of an imaginative writer. I don't want to adjudicate the differences between Orwell and Barthes, but I should note what may not be obvious: They have a shared aesthetic concern with style, a concern that has virtually disappeared from academic discourse.

It should be noted that the hostility or indifference to aesthetic theory and criticism is nothing new. Gerald Graff quotes a scholar in 1901 who scorns attempts to make the study of literature a study of "the work as a work of art":

Why then waste time and brains in thrashing over again something which is after all only subjective opinion? Mere aesthetic theorizing should be left to the magazine writer or to the really gifted critic who feels himself competent to tread in the footsteps of Lessing. My view has always been that the college (university) is a place for research, for scholarship, for finding out something hith-

erto unsuspected. Such is the object of our libraries and our seminary methods. The outside world hasn't the time to investigate; we must do the
investigation.[33]

In trying to put literary study on a scientific basis, Northrop Frye in *The Anatomy of Criticism* (1955) dismissively consigned aesthetic criticism to the capricious history of taste. One must, however, distinguish the grounds for hostility in its various expressions. For the ideology critics, the issue is not the lack of scientific rigor in aesthetic criticism, but rather the mystifying power of aesthetic illusion, its displacement or conceal-ment of political motives. Aesthetic illusion is seen as a kind of cultural pathology.

It has become almost an embarrassment to speak in behalf of aes-thetic value in the academy. One of the few unembarrassed exceptions is the voice of Harold Bloom, whose jeremiad *The Western Canon* begins defiantly with an affirmation of the aesthetic against its demystifiers: "'Aesthetic value' is sometimes regarded as a suggestion of Immanuel Kant's rather than an actuality, but that has not been my experience dur-ing a lifetime of reading." I take it that Bloom is saying that aesthetic value is an experience and not a theory. Indeed, if we insist on a theo-retical justification of the aesthetic, we will end up speaking as does Barbara Herrnstein Smith of its contingent and subjective status (it is in the eye of the beholder and every beholder sees things differently) or we may find that the aesthetic is inescapably contaminated by political, moral, and philosophical interests. Bloom seems to me overconfident, even facile, in his insistence on the purity of aesthetic experience, but he is right to resist theoretical efforts to deny his experience of the sub-lime, which is for him the aesthetic emotion. The theoretical project of aesthetics may prove vulnerable, but its vulnerability is not proof against the actuality of aesthetic experience. There have been persuasive ways of talking and writing about it when confronting a work of art or, for that matter, a work of nature. Louis Armstrong had an instinctive knowledge of the limits of theory and of the actuality of experience when he re-sponded to a request for a definition of jazz by saying that if you have to define it, you'll never know it.

It is true that the teaching of an aesthetic response to literature pres-ents special difficulties. You do not in fact teach an aesthetic response, you practice it. What does it mean to practice it? Certainly not by the application of a method or a set of procedures, but rather by comments, indications, and gestures that accompany interpretation, the staple of literary criticism. Interpretation looks for patterns, significant coherences or incoherences that constitute the meanings of a text, but by itself is not a route to an apprehension of its beauty or power. In the course of an interpretation, the reader should be alert to surprises that reveal the wit, the ingenuity, the imagination of the work, the rightness and splendor of the language. The critic need not, indeed cannot, avoid talking about ethical, political, religious, or historical issues. What is decisive is the way he speaks or writes about the work, the kind of attention he gives to what count as aesthetic qualities. An aesthetic response foregrounds the work and doesn't allow it to be devalued by one or another discourse.

Literary criticism in the aesthetic sense is neither liberal nor conservative, progressive nor reactionary. Aesthetics may attach itself to politics as when fascists aestheticize power, or it may be experienced as a temptation to be avoided as when Lenin refused to listen to Beethoven's music, because he felt it distracted him from the task of making a revolution. But the aesthetic response has no necessary political applications. What may be the case is that there is a temperamental disaffinity between literary and political sensibilities, which could account in part at least for the sense of frustration and exasperation in current debates. Arguments cannot resolve differences between sensibilities.

Literary sensibility is not enough to constitute a discipline, which requires methods that can be exercised by its practitioners and into which its students can be initiated. The method of New Criticism, for all its inadequacies, proved to be an effective vehicle for its practitioners, particularly its most distinguished practitioners. But even in the New Criticism with its disposition toward formulas about paradox and ambiguity, a kind of mechanism of application developed which can easily betray the sensibility. We see this in the routinization of the criticism. In a way, literary criticism thrives to the extent that it resists academic professionalization. Methods and scholarship can produce certain kinds of knowledge about texts, but they are not guarantors of the experience of literary works. What is distressing about the current situation is that a literary sensibility is not requisite for professional entry into the discipline.

It is true that a discipline depends on method, and it may be a reason why the culture of the discipline has always had trouble accommodating the practice of aesthetic criticism. However, as I have already remarked, the current disrepute of, or uninterest in, aesthetic value may have less to do with theoretical disagreement about its constitution and how one might practice aesthetic criticism than with suspicion about its supposed ideological character. The demise of the aesthetic in the academy begins with the shift in focus from the New Critical concern with the individual work of art to the structuralist and poststructuralist attention to the conditions of its production. The structuralist and the poststructuralist (opposed as they are in other respects) care less for what the text says or does (the task of interpretation) than for the putative external factors that determine its existence and effects. From the perspective of the ideology critics, the aesthetic becomes little more than a mystification that conceals political, class, gender, or racial interests. How can we concentrate on the beauty and power of a work of art, if we are always supposed to look around it to discover its ideological biases and hidden motives? God forbid that we should be taken in by the surfaces of the work. Our failure to focus on "the ideology of the aesthetic" (the title of a book by Terry Eagleton) marks us out as naive or mystified.

Even some scholars who ally themselves with the ideology critics share a sense of loss or discomfort. Here is the testimony of George Levine in an introduction to a book entitled *Aesthetics and Ideology:*

This book and this introduction has required that I face directly my own anxieties about what my passion for literature will seem like to the critical culture with which I want to claim alliance. . . . Beginning this book with the language of the affective, the sublime, the aesthetic, I hoped to rescue from the wreckage of the mystified ideal of the beautiful the qualities that allowed for such rich ambivalences. Eliot is anti-Semitic and worse. Arnold is both statist and snob. I wouldn't be without the writings of either of them. That, I recognize, puts me and this book under suspicion.[34]

The passage, I think, reveals more than Levine intends. What are we to make of allies who suspect the motives of a literary critic who employs the language of the affective, the sublime, the aesthetic? Levine's "anxieties" about taking an aesthetic stance in the presence of his ideologically motivated colleagues are so strong that he cannot avoid compromising his formulations about a "very small breathing space [why very small?] of free play and disinterest"[35] to the point of virtually conceding the futility of the effort.

There must be a distinction between aspiration to some impossible ideal dis-interested stance, and the effort to resist, in certain situations, the political thrust of one's own interests in order—in these situations—to keep open to new knowledge of alternative possibilities and to avoid the consequences of simple partisanship. . . . Even if the Arnoldian and Bloomian ideal of intellectual free space is merely utopian and ultimately a mystifying and disguise of actual power, the notion that the university is not or should not try to be fundamen-tally different from partisan political institutions is merely absurd.[36]

One might wonder to the contrary: Is it not absurd to try to rise above the fray (i.e., "partisan political institutions") if the ideal of intellectual free space is mystification? If you wish to make a case for an aspiration to disinterestedness, it is self-defeating to characterize the object of the effort as "impossible," "ultimately mystifying," and a "disguise of ac-tual power."

This is the place to say something about the contentious phrase "po-litical correctness." Quarrels abound about whether it exists, the extent to which it exists, its content if indeed it does exist, and to whom it ap-plies. My understanding of PC is that it does not or should not apply to the content of a position or theory, but rather to the way it is expressed. Evelyn Fox Keller is right to resist the "easy invocation of PC as shorthand for postmodernism, social constructionism, feminism and multicultural-ism,"[37] for it is possible for those who adhere to these doctrines to be open to criticism and to refrain from imposing their views on others. It is also true that those who attack postmodernism may have their own brand of po-litical correctness which they seek to impose on others. Neoconservative critics often display a closeminded vehemence that belies their claim to disinterestedness. Extreme versions of a doctrine on whatever side of the cultural or political spectrum tend to breed an ethos of political correct-ness and their effect may be disproportionate to their actual constituency. These versions have a way of haunting moderate and reasonable expres-sions of, for instance, postmodernism, as Levine's anxieties suggest.

Political correctness implies intimidation, for it places the offender outside the pale. Of course, it is always possible that the experience of

PC is illusory and paranoiac, that it does not correspond to the facts of the case. But the evidence seems compelling when those in sympathy with a particular view find problems with it and experience fear or anxiety that they may offend those who hold the view unambivalently.

What is remarkable about a number of the essays in the Levine anthology is the defensiveness with which the claim of the aesthetic is articulated. Ideological suspicion informs even the best of the essays. Thus Peter Brooks in a fine essay, "What Happened to Poetics?," cites a passage from a prominent New Historicist in which he asks literary scholars to make a choice between two models of study: "[C]ritical research and teaching in the Humanities may be either a merely academic displacement or a genuine academic instantiation of oppositional social and political praxis." Brooks's response is admirable, but not unexceptionable:

The terms in which the choice is posed create a kind of academic melodrama, of the disempowered professional wimp versus the macho resistance hero. Even if we want to align ourselves with the latter, and want to refuse definitively the notion of the critic as a genteel belated Victorian preaching sweetness and light, we may find that his version of the choice plays into the hands of our enemies, and seriously undermines our ability to speak of literature with any particular qualifications for doing so.[38]

The contrast of styles between Brooks and the New Historicist alone should make it clear whom we are to trust. There is little to add to Brooks's incisive characterization of the false choices posed. But it is dismaying that the incisiveness is marred by a wholly unnecessary concessiveness, "even if we want to align ourselves with the latter [the macho resistance hero]." Why, after what Brooks shows us to be false in the New Historicist's formulation, should we want to align ourselves with the latter? And why the concern about "playing into the hands of our enemies"? In citing a different passage from the same hapless critic, Brooks remarks that "one senses that this is material to hide from the eyes of such as Lynne Cheney or Hilton Kramer or Dinesh D'Souza, or other recent critics of the academic humanities, since it so readily confirms their intemperate view that the academy has become a conspiracy of aging Sixties radicals made only slightly dangerous by the fact that their prose can't shoot straight." If it confirms their view, how intemperate is it? This is culture war anxiety.

It may seem captious and ungrateful for me to fault Brooks for what is generally an excellent essay. But it is precisely Brooks's excellence as a critic that makes the reader wonder about the allies he has chosen. There are reasons for him not to associate himself with Cheney, Kramer, and D'Souza, but what are his reasons for allying himself with the crude demystifiers of the aesthetic? With such friends, who needs enemies? (Levine, as I have shown, seems caught in a similar bind.) The only explanation can be that in a state of war one feels that one must choose sides, and there are apparently only two sides to choose from.

The quarrel or tension between ideology and aesthetics bears directly on the possibility of objectivity, for aesthetics in its classic formulation (e.g., Shaftesbury, Kant, Schiller) makes a claim for disinterestedness. As Jerome Stolnitz remarks, summarizing the main aesthetic tradition, we perceive beauty when it is the object of a "disinterested and sympathetic attention . . . and contemplation for its own sake alone [as in] 'the look of the rock,' the sound of the ocean, the colors in the painting."[39] Ideology critics have challenged the claim of disinterestedness on grounds that have to be taken seriously. If all our activities are interest-driven, the plausible view of Nietzsche and William James among others, we cannot at the very least be complacent about assuming the existence of disinterestedness. But again we have the problem of how the issue is formulated. What do we mean by interest and disinterest? Ideology critics tend to see interest in its class or group-bound sense as serving the self or the constituency of which the self is a part. But interest can also be directed toward the cause of justice and the interests of humanity and in that sense can be conceived as aspiring to a value-laden disinterestedness. Disinterestedness, understood in this way, is uncommon, but possible.

In construing interest in the narrow self-interested sense, the ideology critics focus on the social, political, and economic conditions in which certain views arise. The question then becomes what to make of a knowledge of those conditions. Does it demystify the aesthetic theory of Shaftesbury to know that it arose out of a sense of personal "displacement" and "self-division" following the English Revolution?

Henceforth it would be impossible for nobles to inhabit an aristocratic Lebensform regarded in the old, pre-seventeenth-century way as altogether natural, normative and problematic.

Such nobles as Shaftesbury, whose family had risen to power and eminence on the dangerously volatile currents of the Restoration, would thereafter occupy a sphere of contingency and human construction where their status, titles, and house of assembly would conceivably be abolished anew, where the nobles recognize themselves at a deep level as now suffering the sufferance of the people.[40]

This passage describes the circumstances in which Shaftesbury conceived a utopia of aesthetic contemplation, freed of the contingencies of [his] social existence; it does not discredit his ideas. It may be true, as the writer of the passage argues, that "Shaftesbury's double displacement first of the political onto the ethical and then of the ethical onto the aesthetic would effectively obscure in later years the ideological role of his writing in assisting to legitimate the Whig consensual polity."[41] But Shaftesbury's work influenced the work of Kant, Schiller, and the Victorian social critics (it informs Arnold's conception of culture) and cannot be *reduced* to "Whig consensual polity."

I have cited Linda Dowling, whose short and excellent book *The Vulgarization of Art: The Victorians and Aesthetic Democracy* (an essay of only 100 pages) exemplifies what is admirable, but rare, in ideological interpretation. Her account of the conditions under which aesthetic ideas arise illuminates their motives, but does not cause her to prejudge the value of those ideas. Her view of the ideas themselves is complex. She appreciates their character as a moral critique of the constitution of society, particularly in her discussion of Schiller's *On an Aesthetic Education of Man.* Her engagement with the ideas is philosophical rather than ideological, when, for instance, she follows Alasdair MacIntyre in his view of how Shaftesbury's "rejection . . . of the traditional Aristotelian ideas concerning the essential nature and telos of human beings [and his reliance on 'the natural passions of the individual'] makes it henceforth impossible to supply anything like a traditional account of the virtues.'"[42] Dowling's work, influenced by current ideological concerns in the academy, displays the possibility of disinterestedness that is the occasion for her discussion.

There are lessons to be drawn from her account of the aesthetic tradition. From its very beginnings, there has been a tension between its emphasis on distinction (hence its elitism) and its ambition to become the spiritual basis of democracy, an expression of the *sensus communis* in Shaftesbury's phrase. This tension is evident in Arnold's aristocratic conception of cultural distinction, on the one hand, and his view of culture as a force that wishes "to do away with classes," on the other. Arnold wanted to democratize society on his high cultural terms. But democracy cannot exist without the consent of the people, who are formed by a mass culture and who may not be "in communication with the realm of transcendental value"[43] where beauty can be found or who may find beauty in sources other than the transcendental realm (popular culture, for instance). If the aesthetic sense is to have the power not only to express beauty, but to transform social reality (Schiller's view), it can do so only with the consent of the people, otherwise it would become another form of tyranny. We in the academy are the heirs to this unresolvable tension, which may not be an undesirable condition, so long as we understand that it cannot be resolved. The canon will always be under pressure, at once resistant and accommodating to change. The danger arises when the tension becomes a war in which adversaries try to resolve it one way or the other.

So long as this tension remains unresolved, debate will persist. I do not foresee (nor do I think desirable) a return to a time (largely imaginary) when the professional imperative was the contemplation of the aesthetic qualities of a work of art, exclusive of political, historical, and moral considerations—of the sort recently advocated by Harold Bloom in *The Western Canon*. Bloom, it should be remarked, does not deny the political and social dimensions of literary production:

The canons do directly serve the social and political, and indeed the spiritual, concerns of the wealthier classes of each generation of Western society. It seems clear that capital is necessary for the cultivation of aesthetic values. Pindar, the superb last champion of archaic lyric, invested his art in the celebratory exercise of exchanging odes for grand prices, thus praising the wealthy for their generous support of his generous exaltation of their divine lineage. This alliance of sublimity and financial and political power has never ceased, and presumably never can or will.[44]

There are exceptions to the alliance of sublimity and financial and political power (Bloom mentions Blake and Whitman), but he has caught hold of a main truth that G. Wilson Knight anticipated in his discussion of Shakespeare. There is an imperial dimension in the greatest imagina-

tions. Shakespeare's imagination fed on the expansive powers of Eliza-
bethan political and social life, Dante's on the insurgent energies of the
Italian cities in the Renaissance. The political and social are inescapable
in experiencing and understanding the energies of art. Do we demystify
the sublimity in order to show it to be a reflex or function of crude power,
or do we appreciate the *sublimation* of power? Sublimity is the sublimation of power and to the extent that it resists demystification it is an object of aesthetic criticism.

In characterizing the aesthetic tradition, I focused on its major strain,
that of Shaftesbury, Kant, Schiller, and Arnold: the strain of disinterested
contemplation of the beautiful. There are other aesthetic discourses, for
instance, those of Addison and Hogarth, as Ronald Paulson has demon-
strated, that challenge the aesthetics of disinterestedness. In Paulson's
account the aesthetics of Hogarth finds its way not only in Hogarth's
practice as a visual artist, but also in the work of novelists and poets,
among them Henry Fielding, John Cleland, Laurence Sterne, and Oliver
Goldsmith. Even Dr. Johnson opposes the Shaftesburian aesthetic in "its
distancing of art from life." Johnson valued art's involvement with
human life.[45] It would be unfortunate if I was understood as proposing
the aesthetic as a monolith and itself not a field of contention. My own
disposition is more Shaftesburian than Hogarthean. What I am proposing, however, is a revival of interest in aesthetics. Ideology critique has
taken as its object of attack aesthetics itself, not simply its tradition of
disinterested contemplation of the beautiful.

Politics in and of art need not be the object of the demystifier's eye,
searching for motives of domination. In our democratic age we should be
able to appreciate what is valuable in the imagination of an aristocratic
conception of life in the works of the ancient Greek poets or the spiritual aspirations in the religious imaginations of Dante and Milton. It is
not history or politics that is inimical to the artistic imagination, but tendentious and impoverished conceptions of history and politics.

We should also be able to recover an idea of culture which provides
a vantage point to criticize what is corrupt and degraded in contemporary political and social life. The new discipline of cultural studies pro-
motes ideological criticism of what is seen as the pretensions of high
culture. The cause of high culture has been largely taken up by neo-

conservatives outside the academy whose stridency often gives it a sectarian coloration that compromises its spirit. Left and right provoke stridency in each other. Robert Hughes neatly sums up the current situation: "Radical academic and cultural conservatives are now locked in a full-blown, mutually sustaining *folie à deux,* and the only person each dislikes more than the other is the one who tells them both to lighten up."[46] What we need to do is to disengage cultural criticism from the distortions in the current practices of left and right politics.

The vitality of a culture (its literature, music, and art) depends on the capacity of readers, spectators, and listeners to discriminate among their experiences. An intelligent criticism responsive to aesthetic value can instruct and inspire the confidence of artists in their own work. Newspapers, nonacademic and a few academic journals in their cultural columns continue to do the work of appreciation and discrimination with and without distinction.[47] (There is a division between nonacademic journalism and the academy that periodically flares up into outright hostility between them.) Journalism, however, is not a sufficient medium for aesthetic criticism, no matter how gifted some of its practitioners may be. For the most part, journalists lack the scholarship, the training, and the time for the kind of reflection necessary for serious criticism. The corrosive skepticism about aesthetic value in the academy (where the work of serious criticism is supposed to take place) necessarily has a harmful effect on the cultural life. If aesthetic appreciation and discrimination are not thought about and taught in the schools, they are bound to atrophy in the educated population.

Since nothing lasts forever, we might ask what will or should happen when the hermeneutics of suspicion will have exhausted itself and the desire for the pleasures of reading returns to the academy. Will we be able to revive the capacity for aesthetic response, and what form would the revival take? A return to the status quo ante (that is, to the time before the advent of critical theory) is neither possible nor desirable. To the ideology critics, the social theorists, the moral philosophers, the metaphysicians, Harold Bloom urges "a stubborn resistance whose single aim is to preserve poetry as fully and purely as possible."[48] (Poetry in the context of his argument is a synecdoche for the literary work.) But should we resist the political genius of Shakespeare's history plays, or the theological interest of *The Divine Comedy* or *Paradise Lost,* and simply regard it as trope or metaphor? Should we ignore the remarkable sociological and moral imagination of *Middlemarch*? Retrieving the literary from the ideology critics does not require us to return to a time when readers of Eliot, if not of Pound, turned a blind eye to his anti-Semitism or simply discounted it. It does require us to resist our premature impulse to pass moral and political judgment. Literary experience is not a pure thing; it is an amalgam of interests that includes the political, the historical, the ethical, and so on, but not necessarily at the expense of the aesthetic.

My argument represents an ongoing effort on my part to reenfranchise certain ideas that have become disreputable in the humanities: objectivity, disinterestedness, tradition, aesthetic appreciation. I think their loss of credit is a misfortune for the academy. They are or should be the common possession of scholars of whatever political or cultural persuasion: left, right, or center. Which is not to say that it is a bad thing for these ideas to have been put under the kind of pressure that forces a reformulation and strengthening of them. To agree on their necessity in intellectual exchange is not to agree about everything, but it may create the possibility of overcoming the current academic Balkanization in which one always seeks the comfort zone of the like-minded or prepares to do battle with the enemy.

## 2

꩜

# Critics on the Right

"Left" and "right" are an unfortunate legacy of the spatial arrangements of the National Assembly, following the French Revolution. They are not an entirely fair representation of the opposition of forces in our culture wars, certainly not if the Enlightenment has become a bête noire of the left, or if Nietzsche is an inspiration of the cultural left. As Alan Wolfe remarks, "social criticism has become more complicated not only because, on some key issues of the day, left and right have switched sides but also because, on others, there are no coherent sides to switch."[1] Faute de mieux, I refer to the left and right with a caveat that they be enclosed in quotation marks even if they have not been put down on paper.

In characterizing the culture wars, I have devoted my attention to "the cultural left." What are we to say of the critics on the right? What contribution have they made to the wars? Roger Kimball's *Tenured Radicals* and Dinesh D'Souza's *Illiberal Education,* both published in 1990, are forceful examples of the conservative critique of the academy. They embrace the values of tradition, objectivity, and aesthetic appreciation. And they are unembarrassed promoters of the Western canon. They make telling criticisms of the thought and expression of their adversaries and relate devastating anecdotes of intellectual intolerance in the academy. But they write in a spirit devoid of the critical disinterestedness that they advocate. Part of the problem is genre. They have written works of journalism addressed to a wider audience than the academy. Journalistic prose at its best has the virtue of clarity and even of elegance. It can summarize complex thought with an awareness that

35

there is always the risk of reductiveness and oversimplification. And again at its best, it performs the valuable function of what the French call *haute-vulgarization,* making the work of the intellect inside and outside the academy available to an interested public. But journalistic writing is not always at its best. Too often, as in the case of Roger Kimball or Dinesh D'Souza, the writing lacks the decorum of scholarly caution. There is too much reliance on scornful and sarcastic rhetoric, though it is true that a passage like the following seems to invite it.

In the ambivalent world of "not quite/not white," on the margins of metropolitan desire, the *founding objects* of the Western world become the erratic, eccentric, accidental *objéts trouvés* of the colonial discourse—the part-objects of presence. It is then that the body and the book loose [*sic*] their representational authority. Black skin splits under the racist gaze, displaced into signs of bestiality, genitalia, grotesquerie, which reveal the phobic myth of the undifferentiated whole white body.[2]

Words like "ridiculous," "ludicrous," "blather" appear frequently in Kimball's prose with very little indication that he has made a generous effort to fully understand what he is attacking. Marxists, New Historicists, feminists, psychoanalytic critics of every and any persuasion are indiscriminately lumped together to become the objects of polemical animus.

I begin with Roger Kimball. Consider his response to a formulation of Freud's contribution to our understanding of selfhood by the sociologist Nancy Chodorow. Chodorow is a moderate feminist, who values Freud's achievement and has been criticized by more radical feminists who regard Freud as the enemy. (None of this is presented in Kimball's account.) Chodorow writes: "[P]sychoanalysis radically undermines notions about autonomy, individual choice, will, responsibility, and rationality, showing that we do not control our lives in the most fundamental sense."[3] Kimball asks us to "think about this for a moment" and his response has all the marks of only a moment's thought. "In what sense," he asks, "has psychoanalysis really *undermined* the ideas of will, choice, responsibility, etc.? After all, didn't Professor Chodorow *will* to write this essay? Did she not *choose* to contribute to this volume? Did she not assume the *responsibility* of submitting a manuscript by a certain date and so on? Notwithstanding the voluminous attempts of academic psychoanalysts to convince us that we are creatures of unconscious impulses, do we not in fact bear witness to the cogency and pertinence of the concepts every day?"[4] Psychoanalysis has a deterministic view of the psyche, which does not preclude the assumption of responsibility for one's behavior. Indeed, without such responsibility, the practice of psychoanalysis is impossible. In the sentence quoted, Chodorow does not qualify her statement with an account of how Freud imagines responsibility in his conception of determinism, but in the phrase "the most fundamental sense," there is the implication that there may be a less fundamental sense in which autonomy, responsibility, and so on are operative. And indeed if Kimball had read beyond the first page, he would have found the following passage:

Even though Freud radically undermined notions of the unitary and autonomous individual, we can see psychoanalysis, in its endless, reflexive involvement with self-investigation, as a particularly intense scrutiny of the individual, the apogee of the development of individualism in Western culture. . . . Freud . . . wanted to resolve the paradox he created, to use the scrutiny of individual and self not to celebrate fragmentation but to restore wholeness. He could not accept that the self is the outcome of messy unconscious processes and a warring structure, that it disallows individual morality, autonomy and responsibility; he wanted to reconstitute the individual and the self he had dissected.[5]

In any case, Kimball's quarrel is not with Chodorow, but with Freud, who is not a tenured radical. In promoting disinterested inquiry, Kimball has an obligation which he has failed to discharge to treat the Freudian idea seriously rather than flippantly. Which means, among other things, not conflating Freud with cultural radicalism.

Certainly there are sufficient reasons to criticize the academy. Why then should criticism become captious and unjust? When Geoffrey Hartman, the distinguished scholar of romanticism at Yale, declares that Paul de Man's early writing was "more than a theoretical expression of anti-Semitism," Kimball gratuitously remarks: "Meaning, perhaps, that a merely theoretical expression of anti-Semitism isn't such a bad thing."[6] That is not what Hartman is saying. On the contrary, he is rebuking a friend for something more serious than the theoretical expression of anti-Semitism, an endorsement of the views that contributed to the massacre of Jews. One may differ with Hartman's attempt to show that de Man's later work may be an effort to expiate the sins of his youth, but is it necessary to insinuate that Hartman, a refugee from Nazism, regards theoretical anti-Semitism as of little significance? Kimball's animus has taken over and interfered with his sense of justice. As a culture warrior, he scatters his shots indiscriminately.

People are named, follies exposed, substantive issues rarely explored. Relativism, a theoretical bête noire, is simply dismissed with contempt every time it is affirmed by a literary theorist—as if there is no possible legitimacy to the view. Though he acknowledges the talents of his adversaries, Kimball never addresses the question of why they would continue to have such contemptible views. Instead he holds them or their sayings up to ridicule, hardly the most productive use of the critical intelligence. In his conviction of the rightness of his position, he resembles his adversaries who combine self-righteousness with a *theoretical* epistemological modesty (i.e., we are all locked into our perspectives and cannot transcend them).

Which is not to say that Kimball and his fellow conservative critics are never on target. The strength of their work is in the force of their criticism when they are on target. Most troublesome, however, is the poverty of positive ideas in their work. Assume for a moment that the cultural radicals were routed from the academy. What would replace their agenda if their conservative critics had their way? In *To Reclaim a Legacy*, William Bennett invokes Matthew Arnold as the presiding deity for whom culture is "the best that has been thought and said." The humanities are important, Bennett writes, taking his cue from Arnold (or his view of Arnold), because

[t]hey tell us how men and women of our own and other civilizations have grappled with life's enduring, fundamental questions: What is justice? What should be loved? What deserves to be defended? What is courage? What is noble? What is base? . . . These questions are not simply diversions for intellectuals or playthings for the idle. As a result of the ways in which these questions have been answered, civilizations have emerged, nations have developed, wars have been fought, and people have lived contentedly or miserably.

Roger Kimball, who quotes this passage, has corrosive things to say about the rhetoric of the cultural left, but passes over without comment Bennett's platitudes. The real source of the controversy between Bennett and his critics, according to Kimball, is that Bennett advocates "a common culture rooted in the highest ideals of the Western tradition."[7] The implication is that the greatest thinkers and artists in the Western tradition agree about its highest ideals. All is harmony and unity. Deconstruction is the enemy because it "'disturbs' a commitment to the established conventions of Western society and culture, including an allegiance to values such as order, harmony, stability and unity."[8] Kimball's target in this passage is deconstructionist architecture, but what he says applies to the humanities generally. Deconstruction has a lot to answer for, but it is served, not condemned by such an impoverished conception of the tradition posed against it. Not a word about the vital currents and countercurrents that inhabit the tradition. When I think of the Western tradition, I think of its opposing currents, the oppositions between Plato and Nietzsche, Rousseau and his fellow philosophers, T. S. Eliot and Milton, Adam Smith and Marx. The Western tradition is a dialectic, a scene of struggle, not a set of coherent ideals. It is not that Bennett and Kimball are ignorant of the conflicts within the tradition. They are willing to sacrifice their knowledge of those conflicts for polemical purposes. A sort of complacent attitude about the tradition pervades their work.

It is worth staying with Arnold to consider the uses to which he has been put in the culture wars. Arnold's critical method is at its weakest in "The Study of Poetry," where he ranks and fixes the stars in the literary heavens (Shakespeare, Homer, Dante, et al.), each touchstone getting several lines about what constitutes his supreme greatness. There are a number of objections to Arnold's touchstones. The few lines that he gives to each of the classics hardly makes a case for them. The assumption perhaps is that the case has already been made in the long tradition of their acceptance (Arnold is stating what is the case, not creating the tradition), so only a few lines are needed to make necessary discriminations, for instance, the discrimination that Chaucer lacks the high seriousness of supreme greatness. There is also the failure to take into account changes in the way the tradition has been perceived, a consideration that informs Eliot's "Tradition and the Individual Talent." Arnold's exclusion of Chaucer from his touchstones and Eliot's early hostility to Milton show how historically determined certain judgments are. And what of the tensions and conflicts between the classics that compose the canon, conflicts that may lead to an antagonism to a work, even to a desire to expel it from the canon? This becomes even clearer when one moves beyond literature to philosophy and political theory. Nietzsche is the enemy of Socrates, Marx the enemy of Adam Smith, Kierkegaard the enemy of Hegel. To be sure, a great adversary may be necessary to the development of one's genius. Nietzsche needed Socrates to think his ideas, so they belong together in the pantheon. But Bennett's Arnoldian phrase, endorsed by Kimball, "a common culture rooted in the highest ideals of the Western tradition," obscures the passionate conflicts between great writers and their highest ideals. Of all the conservative critics it is Allan Bloom who has best understood and presented the fact that the Western tradition is a scene of conflict, not a set of coherent ideals.

The best of Arnold is the critic capable of thinking against himself. In "The Function of Criticism at the Present Time," Arnold praises Edmund Burke, for his courageous willingness to reconsider his view of the French Revolution in light of the reality it had produced. "Burke's return upon himself" can be a motto for Arnold's best work. The neoconservative appropriation of Arnold doesn't sufficiently appreciate Arnold's "return upon himself."

In 1994 Yale University Press published a new edition of Matthew Arnold's *Culture and Anarchy* edited by Samuel Lipman, the late publisher of the neoconservative periodical *The New Criterion*. The edition includes essays that are not of a conservative cast, for instance, those of Steven Marcus and Gerald Graff, but Lipman's essay suggests a special affinity between Arnold and the conservatives.

It is not hard to see why Matthew Arnold has become the intellectual property of conservatives: He stands for all the values denigrated by the cultural left, such as disinterestedness, aesthetic autonomy, and authority (the original title of *Culture and Anarchy* was *Authority and Anarchy*). Arnold is a good source for those who wish to combat left-wing cant, surpassed only by George Orwell. And he provides support for conservative vigilance about social unrest. Here is Arnold who saw the working class of nineteenth-century England: "raw and half-developed . . . long lain half-hidden amidst its poverty and squalor . . . now issuing forth from its hiding place to assert an Englishman's heaven-born privilege of doing as he likes, meeting where it likes, bawling what it likes, [and] breaking what it likes."[9] This is the Arnold of law and order, concerned with the *effect* of anarchy on society who could quote with approval his father's words: "As for rioting, the old Roman way of dealing with *that* is always the right one, flog the rank and file, and fling the leaders from the Tarpeian Rock."[10]

There is, of course, another Arnold, whose compassion for the poor moved him to indignation. In "The Function of Criticism at the Present Time," Arnold answers the triumphalists of the Industrial Revolution with a murmuring refrain, "Wragg is in custody." Against the trumpeting of "our unrivaled" happiness by the eulogists of the Industrial Revolution, Arnold evokes a scene of "grimness, bareness, and hideousness . . . the workhouse, the dismal Mapperly Hills—how dismal those who have seen them will remember—the gloom, the smoke, the strangled illegitimate child!"[11]

The illegitimate child is still with us and in great numbers. The neoconservative refrain is louder than a murmur, and the target of its wrath is the welfare state. Of course, it was not the welfare state that created Wragg, but a version of the unregulated industrial system that the conservatives (liberals, in Arnold's day) promote. Conservatives speak of moral responsibility and exhort us to read and practice the Book of Virtues. So did the Victorian critics. But the object of their moral passion was broader than that of our conservatives. Arnold found moral irresponsibility in all the classes: aristocratic, middle, and working. The cardinal sin of the upwardly mobile middle class (Arnold's principal audience) was and still is its passion for accumulating wealth. The neoconservative ethic revives the Calvinist gospel mercilessly exposed by George Eliot in her characterization of Bulstrode in *Middlemarch*, a gospel glorifying the virtues of capital accumulation. The Victorian social critics viewed the spirit of laissez-faire (what Arnold disparagingly called "doing as one likes" and what modern conservatives approvingly call "the free market") as destructive of the moral fabric of society.

Arnold affirms the state as an expression of the best self, and Samuel Lipman, from a conservative perspective, is quick to note a failure in Arnold "to see that the state bore within itself a monstrous tyranny."[12] Lipman has in mind modern totalitarianism in its Nazi and Stalinist incarnations. Of course, the threat in Arnold's time was not totalitarianism, but the misery of the masses. The captains of industry did not offer a solution to the social problem and neither did civil society, the intermediate institutions like the Church that stand between the person and the State. In turning to the State, Arnold, Carlyle, and Ruskin left an ambiguous legacy: on the one hand, a law and order rhetoric that liberals and radicals find repressive, and on the other, a justification for necessary political reforms like the regulation of child labor and social security (all the components of the welfare society that constitute the safety net). Staunch supporters of law and order, the conservatives have as their real target the tyranny that might result from revolutionary or even reformist passion. "The conservative revolution," the mantra of Newt Gingrich and his colleagues, is an unremarked oxymoron. Conservative arguments against state intervention to create social reform employ the metaphor of the slippery slope. It is at least a question of whether the logic of social welfare is tyranny or, worse, totalitarianism.

In their attack on the travesties of the cultural left (its ways of politicizing all discourse), the neoconservatives have adopted the stance of disinterestedness. Lipman cites with approval Arnold's caveat to the cultured individual:

Neither . . . is public life and direct political action permitted to him. For it is his business . . . to get the present believers in action, and lovers of political talking and doing, to make a return upon their own minds, scrutinize their stock actions and habits much more, value their present talking and doing much less; in order that, by learning to think more clearly, they may come at last to act less confusedly.[13]

Lipman is right to chastise Arnold for compromising this admirable ideal by uncritically affirming the State. But shouldn't the same strictures apply to neoconservatives who have uncritically adopted the stock habits of thought associated with free market capitalism? History may have shown that conservatives are right in their advocacy of the free market as a necessary condition of social and political vitality, but they have not been sufficiently sensitive to the variety of forms it takes in different societies, the ways in which it can be qualified to mitigate its casualties. (Every system has casualties.)

One doesn't have to agree with the cultural left that the claim to disinterestedness is always a case of ideological mystification to find a lack
of disinterestedness in the neoconservative defense of it. Disinterestedness implies the capacity for self-criticism; what is missing across the
cultural spectrum is the habit of thinking against oneself. The result may
be failure to take into account the complication in the view one holds.
Consider Peter Shaw's criticism of Harold Bloom's defense of the Western literary canon. It is not enough that Harold Bloom defends it, for
Shaw its defense must also mean, as it does not for Bloom, a defense of
the West and its tradition of what he calls rational thought. But the
canon is not a homogeneity of "rational" thinking. (Does Shaw mean rationalist thinking?) It accommodates quarrels between the rationalist
Plato and the immoralist Nietzsche, between Enlightenment liberalism
and Burkean conservatism, between the Augustan affirmation of Reason and the Romantic celebration of the imagination. The energies of art
are often subversive and not easily contained within a canon, which is
a term of theological orthodoxy. In "The Function of Criticism at the Present Time," Arnold acknowledges and values what might even be dangerous in the intellectual and imaginative life. "It must be apt to study and
praise elements that for the fulness of spiritual perfection are wanted,
even though they belong to a power which in the practical sphere may
be maleficent."[14] The fact that liberalism and radicalism have developed
their own pieties does not justify an opposing set of pieties. If we accept
Arnold's characterization of the essential activity of the cultured mind as
thinking against oneself, an activity imperfectly realized in Arnold's own
thought (and one suspects in anyone's thought), we can begin to appreciate how both our cultural left and our cultural right mirror each other in
their tendentiousness. It is impossible and undesirable always to resist
the temptation of politics. Arnold himself is proof of the impossibility.
But the life of the mind depends on its capacity to resist the temptation
and its refusal to sacrifice itself to the cause of party or ideology.

For all of Roger Kimball's faults, he is not without critical ability.
Many of his examples of current critical practice deserve his severity.
Like Kimball, D'Souza scores effectively against vulnerable targets, but
he can misunderstand some of his targets egregiously, and his own approach to literature is obtuse and even perverse. For example, D'Souza

provides an epigraph from Aristotle for his chapter on affirmative action: "It is thought that justice is equality, but not for all persons, only those who are equal." D'Souza does not give the source of the quotation nor the context, but it is reasonable to surmise that Aristotle meant to exclude women and slaves from the condition of equality. What an unfortunate way of introducing an attack on affirmative action, for not only are we provoked to speculate about D'Souza's motives in attacking affirmative action, we also wonder about what he values in the classical tradition.

In attacking affirmative action, D'Souza poses "diversity of minds" against the prevailing multicultural model of ethnic diversity. It is true that ethnic diversity does not necessarily encourage intellectual diversity. In viewing the mind as determined by its ethnicity or race, one encourages homogeneity of outlook in every ethnic group. (An example of this is Derrick Bell's admonition to black colleagues about the dangers of being black and thinking white.) But it doesn't follow from the tendentious uses to which ethnicity and race have been put that they have been disqualified as subjects for inquiry. The individual in his or her individuality is not an abstraction from the influences that form a life. D'Souza is simply not interested in the ways ethnicity and race inflect one's outlook on life. The fact is that diversity is not a compelling value for D'Souza. "Although university leaders speak of the self-evident virtues of diversity, it is not at all obvious why it is necessary to a first-rate education. Universities such as Brandeis, Notre Dame, and Mount Holyoke, which were founded on principles of religious or gender homogeneity, still manage to provide an excellent education."[15] One needs first to remark D'Souza's scholarly carelessness. Brandeis and Notre Dame were founded by Jews and Catholics, respectively, but neither institution was "founded on principles of religion." Brandeis, where I teach, is a secular institution open to students of all religious, racial, and ethnic backgrounds. Notre Dame has a religious orientation, but it too is open to students of every background. It is true, however, that Brandeis in practice tends toward an ethnic (not a religious) homogeneity in its student population. This is rightly seen by administration and faculty of all political persuasions as a problem. There are distinct educational advantages (social as well as intellectual) in being among other students from a variety of backgrounds. D'Souza is blind to the reality.

He displays a vulgar understanding of literary study past and present, as in the following passage.

Much of modern literary criticism is based on the surprising premise that poems and novels do not mean anything in particular; they do not correspond to any specific "reality," either material or metaphysical. Jacques Lacan, who has greatly influenced *au courant* criticism, wrote that modern interpretation rejects from the outset the commonsensical belief that objects exist independently of ourselves in the external world, and that our information about them is generally reliable. The genesis of this approach is probably Austin Warren and Rene Wellek's influential book *A Theory of Literature* (1949), which maintained that the definition of literature was problematic and posited circumstances under which Shakespeare might be displaced by the Manhattan phone book or by graffiti.[16]

I don't know of a critic of any standing in the field who would claim that poems and novels do not mean anything in particular. A New Critic might claim that a work has multiple meanings, a reader-centered critic might claim that he or she constitutes the meaning of the text in the act of reading or, in another version, engages in a transaction with the structure of the text to produce meaning, a deconstructionist might speak of being undecided about the meanings of a text. D'Souza shows little understanding of what is involved in the question of the possible relationships between literature and reality. No critic believes in the strict correspondence between a work and reality. While acknowledging a relationship between art and life, critics quarrel, unsurprisingly, about the nature of the relationship. It diminishes the imagination not to recognize its capacity to invent a world or to mediate or transform the world external to it. Deconstructionists speak of the gap between text and the world and the illusion of reference, but that view, contrary to D'Souza's, does not define modern criticism. Finally, we have D'Souza's travesty of Wellek and Warren's *Theory of Literature* and his unsubstantiated, indeed impossible to substantiate, claim that they are responsible for what is wrong with modern criticism, because they maintained the reasonable view that the definition of literature is problematic. Lest there be any doubts as to where Wellek and Warren stand on "the definition of literature," the following passage from the introduction to *The Theory of Literature* should dispel them:

We must beware of both false relativism and false absolutism. Values grow out of the historical process of valuation, which they in turn help us to understand. The answer to historical relativism is not a doctrinaire absolutism which appeals to "unchanging human nature" or the "universality of art." We must rather adopt a view for which the term "Perspectivism" seems suitable. We must be able to refer a work of art to the values of its own time and of all the periods subsequent to its own. A work of art is both "eternal" (i.e., preserves a certain identity) and "historical" (i.e., passes through a process of traceable development). Relativism reduces the history of literature to a series of discrete and hence discontinuous fragments, while most absolutisms serve either only a passing present-day situation or are based (like the standards of the New Humanists, the Marxists, and the Neo-Thomists) on some abstract non-literary ideal unjust to the historical variety of literature. "Perspectivism" means that we recognize that there is one poetry, one literature, comparable in all ages, developing, changing, full of possibilities. Literature is neither a series of unique works with nothing in common nor a series of works enclosed in time-cycles of Romanticism or Classicism, the age of Pope and the age of Wordsworth. Nor is it, of course, the "block-universe" of sameness and immutability which an older Classicism conceived as ideal. Both absolutism and relativism are false; but the more insidious danger today, at least in the United States, is a relativism equivalent to an anarchy of values, a surrender of the task of criticism.[17]

It should be noted that if D'Souza were right, he could hardly hold the radicals of the 1960s responsible for all that has gone wrong in the academy. Wellek and Warren's book published in 1949 is hardly the work of cultural radicals.

When D'Souza writes of T. S. Eliot, Robert Penn Warren, John Crowe Ransom, and Cleanth Brooks (among the most distinguished of *modern* critics) as upholding a "standard of literary judgment based upon the text itself, independent of external influence," he betrays the fact that he has at best only superficially read their criticism. It is true that the kind of ideological reduction of the literary work that is endemic to literary study today would have been inimical to the understanding shared by the modern critics of literary standards and judgment. But independence of external influence is an impossibility, as their practice shows.

And then there are non sequiturs. One can quarrel with Stanley Fish's view of *Paradise Lost* as an occasion for fumbling readings of the text which remind the reader of his fallen state without concluding, as

D'Souza does, that it "raises the prospect of interpretive nihilism." It is
not a matter of agreeing or disagreeing with Fish (I am in fundamental
disagreement with him); it is a matter of doing justice to your adversary
in the act of disagreeing with him.[18]

If D'Souza is not to be trusted in his account of academic criticism,
he is even less to be relied on as guide to the classics. Here is his account of what they can provide for young people of college age:

A survey of [the classics] immediately suggests that many of them are fully aware
of, and treat with great subtlety, the problems of prejudice, ethnocentrism, and
human difference. Long before Willie Horton raised, in American minds, the
specter of a dark-skinned man sexually assaulting a white woman, Iago raised
this possibility with Brabantio. Will he allow his "fair daughter" to fall into "the
gross clasps of a lascivious Moor"? If he does not intervene, Iago warned, "you'll
have your daughter covered with a Barbary horse." *Othello* and *Merchant of
Venice*, Shakespeare's Venetian plays, are both subtle examinations of nativism
and ethnocentrism. Both engage issues of ethnic and sexual difference. They
reflect a cosmopolitan society's struggle to accommodate the alien, while main-
taining its cultural identity. *Othello* is the tragedy of a foreign warrior who de-
pended on Desdemona's love to legitimate his full citizenship in his new
country—when Iago casts that love into doubt, not just his marriage, but his
identity was fundamentally threatened. By contrast with Othello, Shylock is the
outsider who refused to integrate, and pressed his principles into uncompro-
mising conflict with those of Christian civilization. These timeless examples of
the tension between community and difference are precisely what young people
today should confront, and respond to in terms of their experience.[19]

D'Souza appears to be engaged in a kind of anachronistic multicultural
reading of *Othello* that is unresponsive to the power of the play: its
treatment of the theme of jealousy. Who are the nativists and who the
ethnocentrists? And what makes for its subtlety? D'Souza's anachronistic reading extends to his characterization of *The Merchant of Venice*
as a study in assimilation and the resistance to it. If Shylock had wanted
to "integrate" himself into the community, he would have to convert to
Christianity. This is not integration in the modern sense. D'Souza's use
of the word "integrate" betrays a lack of moral and critical sensitivity.
What D'Souza calls "the tension between community and difference" is
a euphemism for the play's anti-Semitism, which requires an informed

and sensitive historical approach. To speak of *Othello* and *The Merchant of Venice* as timeless examples is cant.

I cite once again Robert Hughes's remark: "Radical and cultural conservatives are now locked in a full-blown, mutually sustaining folie à deux." This is bound to occur when the cultural life of which the academy is an essential part is transformed into a political or ideological battleground. Intellectual debate is of course necessary and vital in the academy and outside it; its focus, when fruitful, is on the quality of argument: the logic, evidence, and ingenuity with which an argument is made. It also requires an openness in adversaries to persuasion. The conditions for such debate do not presently exist. The ideologues of the left provoke the counter ideologues of the right. An excuse for intellectual contempt is provided by embarrassing arguments made on either side of the barricades, most of the embarrassment coming from the left. But there is very little effort made to seek out the strength of the adversary on either side for fear that one's own position might be weakened. The fact is, as Mill and Nietzsche both knew, that intellectual strength comes from exercising your mind against a strong adversary. War, rather than debate, is encouraged by a media view that one gains attention by the aggressiveness with which you make your arguments, not by a scrupulous attention to the arguments of others while you make your own. Something of a military mindset is at work in the no-holds-barred attack on your adversary. The spirit of this mindset is vividly conveyed in a review of a recent book of mine critical of the cultural left in which the reviewer, while grudgingly praising parts of my book, said it would have been much stronger if I had called Richard Rorty an idiot and Louis Althusser, the Marxist structuralist, a wife murderer. As I say, the conditions for fruitful intellectual exchange do not exist at present. One can only hope that they be restored.

3

☙☙

# The Uncanny Canon

In any discussion of literary study, the question of the canon is unavoidable, for it is the question of what we should be teaching our students. Canon is sometimes used interchangeably with tradition, but as a term derived from theology, it differs from tradition. Whereas canon implies fixity and permanence, tradition entails change as well as continuity. I have always been uneasy with "canon" precisely because of its theological connotations. It gives off the odor of sanctity that is not conducive to critical thinking. Or it once gave off the odor of sanctity. No longer inscribed in stone, the canon has become a changing content. New canons have arisen as alternatives to the traditional one: canons of women, African American, or gay and lesbian writers. The term no longer seems authoritarian; it has become elastic and accommodating of diversity.

Controversy, however, persists about the status of the traditional Western canon and the classics that compose it. In a recent article, Garry Wills argues that the Greek and Roman classics ("the core of the old canon for so much of Western history") are neither irrelevant nor repressive as some critics of the cultural left say, but then turns on their conservative defenders and argues that "multiculturalism, far from being a challenge to the classics, is precisely what is reviving them."[1] Wills in effect restates a familiar view that what makes a classic is its capacity to renew itself in every age. "The Enlightenment Homer looked a lot like Alexander Pope, as the Romantic period's Homer looked like Ossian." Wills's advocacy of the classic betrays the anxiety of recent years about its relevance. If the classic does not speak to our immediate concerns, then it can make no urgent claim on our attention. We make a classic relevant by projecting our interests into the work. Every reading becomes a reading of ourselves. What appears to be a defense of the classic is a diminishment of it.

If Homer is like Pope in the eighteenth century and like Ossian in the nineteenth, who is Homer, what distinguishes him from Pope and Ossian? The capacity of a classic to renew itself depends on a more complex conception of it than Wills provides. In reading Homer, we may, of course, find ourselves in him. In which case we should reverse the identification Wills makes and say that both Pope and Ossian in certain respects look like Homer. But a classic may resist the interests and fashions of the age, even offend against them, and yet persist in being lively to us because of the imagination, intelligence, and force of the resistance. What is more foreign to our pacifism than Homer's celebration of Achilles' wrath or to our humanism than Swift's or Nietzsche's misanthropy? This resistance forces us to examine what we have perhaps repressed in ourselves—our own bloody-mindedness that revels in spectacles of mayhem or our distaste for most human encounters. (We encounter bloody-mindedness and bloody acts daily on the TV screen, but in a form that doesn't challenge us to reflect upon our capacity for mayhem. *The Iliad* does.) A classic does not necessarily convert us to its form of wisdom, but if it possesses the power implied by its status in the culture, it forces us to think about our resistance to it and to strengthen or overcome that resistance.

Wills's conception of the classic (which he shares with other recent commentators) dissolves its core identity, so that it becomes whatever its readers wish to make it.

The ancient texts have become eerily modern in what they have to say about power relationships between men and women, gay men and war, superiors and subordinates. They have made Sappho our contemporary. They are rewriting the history of the novel. They raise again the issues of empire, democracy, alliances. When Robert Kennedy read Pericles' funeral oration, they took it as a commission to the best and the brightest. Modern scholars tend to see in it the ominous arrogance of empire.[2]

The ancient texts do indeed have their say about power relationships between men and women, love between men (they knew nothing of gay men), and master–slave, superior–subordinate relationships, but what they say is usually not "eerily modern." Thucydides on the destruction of Melos may have resembled modern indignation about the cruelty of empire, but the contempt of the Homeric hero for Thersites, the common soldier in the ranks of the Greeks, railing against his masters has nothing of the modern democratic sensibility. Nor does Athena's adjudication of the conflict between the furies and Orestes in *The Oresteia* in which the verdict, favoring Orestes, affirms the rule of men over women.

Wills's justification is in the spirit of those on the cultural left who assert that "major canonical texts are not inherently reactionary and that they contain implicit images and models which transcend their immediate historical context and which later readers can respond to."[3] Such a view allows no room for the challenges that a great reactionary work by Swift or DeMaistre or T. S. Eliot might offer to a modern liberal reader. (In speaking of "transcend[ing] their immediate historical context," Wills appears to go against the prevailing historicism which views all talk about transcendence with suspicion. Transcendence in this context, however, is not the timelessness of the classic, but rather its plasticity, that is, its capacity to adapt itself to every age.)

If education is a discovery of things one doesn't already know, we should not be looking in the works we read for a reflection of our own already formed understandings. If we do so, we may never hear the voices that speak a language that addresses our convictions in unfamiliar ways and perhaps unsettles them. Openness to a work does not mean piety. It implies mutual respect between work and reader in which they judge each other, so to speak. A work, of course, is not a living person. It is awakened in the mind of the reader through an act of interpretation and in the process becomes amiable or difficult, interesting or boring in the way people become to one another. A reader may decide that a particular classic is not for him, that it is deficient in rewards—not, however, before the work has been given a chance. Its alienness should not be a mark against it. Like Marlow in *Heart of Darkness*, who to his astonishment finds himself responding to the menacing howls that he hears in the African wilderness (the howls are repressed voices in himself), the most rewarding reading of a work is finding the uncanny in it: that is, its alienness, which corresponds to something in ourselves from which we are estranged and to which we may become reconciled. The shock of recognition is not the facile confirmation of what is already present to our consciousness, but the more difficult realization of what we have ignored or denied or repressed in our lives. I agree with Harold Bloom's answer to the question of what makes works canonical: "The answer, more often than not, has turned out to be strangeness, a mode of originality that either cannot be assimilated, or that so assimilates us that we cease to see it as strange. . . . When you read a canonical work for a first time you encounter a stranger, an uncanny startlement rather than a fulfillment of expectations."[4]

The demand for relevance is pernicious, if what is usually meant by it is immediate relevance. Of course, a work if it is to live for a reader has to touch or move him—in a word, be relevant to his experience—but a reader must also train or prepare himself for the experience by "suspending disbelief" when he encounters an imaginative world based on assumptions different from his own. I taught George Herbert's poems to students unfamiliar with the religious environment of the poems. In the course of our discussion of "The Collar," they could identify themselves with the experience of the speaker's rebellion and appreciate the reversal at the end when the Lord admonishes his "child" and the speaker submits to "my Lord." But to pass to this experience, they had to traverse the Christian symbolism of the poem and in effect discover the possibilities of their experience in the symbolism. The effect was to give a new resonance to their familiar experience with parental authority and adolescent rebellion.

Does the uncanniness of the classic apply only to its first reading? One might find new strangeness on a second reading. It took more than two readings for me to begin to grasp Marlow's puzzling ambivalence toward Kurtz, magnificent idealist and mass murderer (indeed to comprehend the paradox of Kurtz's existence), and to experience the demand it makes on me. And even the first discoveries, if they are profound, have to be rediscovered. The New Critics made much of paradox and ambiguity but did not adequately explain why they are value terms in the appreciation of poetry. Paradox is not merely cleverness, a puzzle to the intellect. It has as one of its meanings heterodoxy—against received doxa, which is one way we get to unorthodox truths—such as Wordsworth's paradox that the child is father of the man, a phrase that contains the whole of the Freudian project. The reader who approaches a work with the aim of demystifying it is quite different from the open reader who may be discovering himself in the strangeness of the classic. The unmasking critic possesses a set of ideological convictions against which he tests, so to speak, the political or moral or psychological value of the work. He judges it against contemporary standards of decency or sophistication, effectively closing himself to the work. The unmasking critic tends to regard the canon and the classics that constitute it with a generalized mistrust—as if the canon was an imperial conspiracy to dominate the mind and not to open it.

What motivates the resistance to the classic? There is a populist disposition (particularly strong in America) toward what is accessible and congenial. The difficulty of a classic has to be made familiar and enjoyable in order to be appreciated. Difficulty is elitist, an offense to the democratic spirit. It is something of a paradox that this populist view is often expressed in an arcane academic language that is itself the source of difficulty, and its expression may reflect a condescension toward the constituencies it wishes to protect. In saying that it is "repressive" to "force . . . a Latino or Thai in Los Angeles, a Puerto Rican in New York, an inner-city African American in either city to read only *King Lear*, *Great Expectations* and other works from the old canon,"[5] Hillis Miller, a critic who throughout his career has addressed himself to works from the old canon, unwittingly fortifies ethnocentric prejudice against what is other, difficult, and strange. It is as if members of ethnic groups need to be protected because of their perceived incapacity to respond to what is not immediately accessible. (Writing about this statement by Miller, Denis Donoghue notes the exaggeration in Miller's use of words like "forcing" and "only."[6] Some curricula require such courses, others simply create opportunities to take the courses, no curricula require only courses in the old canon.)

In 1975 before multiculturalism achieved its ascendancy, Frank Kermode, following T. S. Eliot, could speak of the classic and empire as "closely interwoven" without embarrassment. Nowadays, the connection puts the classic under suspicion, since empire suggests domination. The demystifying critic is now disposed to find motives of domination in the classic text. For Eliot, empire had a different meaning. "Eliot was, in the special sense to which I shall hereafter limit the word, an imperialist: 'I am all for empires,' he once remarked."[7] Empire, in Kermode's use of the word, signifies a cosmopolitan "amplitude and catholicity," the opposite of provinciality. For Charles-Augustin Sainte-Beuve, the great French critic of the nineteenth century, the prime example of the classic (indeed, the one absolute classic) was Virgil, because "his manners were [incomparably] mature, his style, in its complexity and simplicity, is such that only Dante and Racine among the moderns approach him"(22). Virgil's classic status does not make him the greatest poet. "That we refer our culture to him and not to Homer is not an accident but a necessity of history. Ithaca is small, but Rome is Rome; and every nation that has sprung from Rome has always kept it in view . . . 'Virgile est le poete du Capitole'"(17). This is Saint-Beuve's view of the matter, from which his contemporary English admirer, Matthew Arnold, dissented not because he disagreed with Sainte-Beuve's cosmopolitan standard, but rather because he found Virgil inadequate to it. Sainte-Beuve, Arnold, and Eliot, whatever their disagreements, believed that the large "imperial" vision of a classic ("imperial" in a special sense) gave it "perpetual contemporaneity," the distinguishing characteristic of a classic. Their bête noire was "provinciality." Whereas Sainte-Beuve sought the cure for it in Latin antiquity, Arnold turned to Hellenism. "Eliot, like Sainte-Beuve, was faithful to the Latin tradition"(20). Cosmopolitanism may be a feature of every canonical construction, though disagreement about claims for classic status of a particular work is always possible. (Both Arnold and Saint-Beuve would have found current talk about multiple canons of ethnic or racial groups unintelligible.)

This "imperial" way of talking about the classic has become disreputable. Kermode notes the change in thinking about the classic that has taken place. "The law of the *imperium* was like that of the Puritans, powerful, persistent, yet requiring to be broken in the New World . . . [The classic] is perpetual, only its dispositions changing; yet there is a modern empire, founded in the West by that 'handful of half-starved fanatics,' which will reject this classic perpetuity and, changing essentially, make an art which is itself an art of change"(113). Kermode's essay turns to the Old World of Roland Barthes and his cult of the reader, which "liberates" the text from the author's intention by announcing his death. The text becomes the plurality of its readers, no interpretation experiencing the obligation to find common ground with other readers. It is not hard to see the line of development to multiculturalism in which provinciality is transvalued into the particularity of group identity, resisting the universalism of the classic *imperium*.

So the seeds of the dissolution of the cosmopolitan classic are contained in the very condition of modernity. In 1975, Kermode writes with sympathy for this modern development, but not without a certain ambivalence. The maturity and sophistication of his style suggests an unsurmounted affinity with the cosmopolitan ideal. In Kermode's recent writings, one finds an unambivalent disenchantment with modern developments.

The "perpetual contemporaneity" of the classic assumes an objective identity that may vary in its effects over time. Kermode cites the work of E. D. Hirsch, who locates the source of objective meaning in the author. By finding "the best meaning" of the text in authorial intention, Hirsch means to free it from "its imprison[ment] in our culture"(77). A paradoxical phrase, for we normally think of a work embedded in its historical context and the reader's interpretation a possible act of liberation, freeing the text from its embeddedness. Kermode assimilates this view to the imperial classic. ". . . [Hirsch's] 'meaning' is very like 'essence,' and his 'significance' like 'disposition,' so that we are once again back to the imperial classic, its meaning somehow timeless, its significances apprehensible in the aspect of time, though only by an act of divination." Hirsch's distinction between meaning (the objective expression of authorial intention) and significance enables him to "distinguish between things, interesting or silly that people say about texts, and what the texts really mean"(78). Kermode doesn't endorse this view, but in presenting it, he implies what is lost when we regard a text simply as the sum of all appropriations readers make of it. The work loses its separate integrity.

Kermode's example is *Wuthering Heights,* and he singles out Q. D. Leavis's study of the novel as dwarfing all other critical discussions of the novel. Mrs. Leavis sorts out the various strands in the novel (Heathcliff as the Edmund figure from *King Lear*, Heathcliff as the prince transformed into a beast in a fairy story, the Romantic incest story as brother–lover, a sociological novel) only to set them aside for what she regards as the "human centrality" of the novel: "the contrast between the two Catherines, the one willing her own destruction, the other educated by experience and avoiding the same fate"(132). Kermode passes two kinds of judgment on Mrs. Leavis's essay. He finds it superior to all other essays on *Wuthering Heights* ("in its mature authority [it] dwarfs all others"), but at the same time he rejects the privilege it claims for itself as the true reading of the novel ("a reader's share in the novel is not so much a matter of knowing, by heroic efforts of intelligence and divination, what Emily Brontë really meant . . . as of responding creatively to indeterminacies of meaning inherent in the text and possibly enlarged by the action of time" [134]). Kermode is describing a tension in reading between the claim of permanence and the claim of mutability. I think of it as a shifting tension, depending on critical temperament and circumstance. When he wrote his essay in the 1970s, Kermode favored the creative response to indeterminacies. If he were writing the essay now, he would doubtless support the belief that "there is a substance that prevails, however powerful the agents of change"(134), given the critical abuses that have taken place under the aegis of indeterminacy. In the very judgment he passes on Mrs. Leavis's superiority, Kermode affirms "the substance that prevails."

It has become disreputable to speak of objective meaning. According to the prevailing view, objectivity is illusion, subjectivity reality: Our responses to works of literature are ineluctably subjective. We might still ask: Does the individuality of reader response, in many cases the incommensurability of responses (Harold Bloom and I may value a classic in different ways) mean that the value of a classic is a purely subjective affair? If interests vary among readers, and in readers with the passage of time, and if interest determines value, how can we speak of the objective or universal value of anything? Here is Barbara Herrnstein Smith's influential view of the consequences of the variability of readers and their interests. "The fact that Homer, Dante and Shakespeare do not figure significantly in the personal economies [of many people], do not perform individual or social functions that gratify their interests, *do not have value for them* might be taken as qualifying the claims of transcendent universal value made for such works. As we know, however, it is routinely taken instead as evidence or confirmation of the cultural deficiency—or, more piously, "deprivation"—of such people."[8]

We should not routinely dismiss indifferent or hostile responses to a classic as signs of cultural deficiency, but neither should we dismiss the possibility that this might be the case. One might ask the following questions: Who are these many people for whom Homer, Dante, and Shakespeare do not have value? Have they read their works in or out of school? Have they seen Shakespeare performed? If not, then the case against the value of the classics is trivial. We cannot know whether Homer has value unless he has been experienced. The more interesting case would be those who have experienced Homer and reject him. But rejection in this case is not decisive, because it may reflect inadequacy in the readers or spectators. And we would know whether the failure lies with the work or the reader only by evaluating the quality of the reader's response. Of course, here lies the rub. One can imagine Smith's objection to the elitism of evaluating the responses of those who do not find value in the classics. The objection might have force if evaluation were not ecumenical and did not include those who say they do find value. Unearned arrogance and arbitrariness are always possible in the making of evaluations. We need therefore to distinguish between scrupulous and irresponsibly arbitrary judgment. But evaluation is an inescapable function of intelligence, and pedagogy would not be possible without it. Smith speaks of "the most fundamental character of literary value" as "its mutability and diversity" in disparaging the "humanist's fantasy of transcendence, endurance and universality" as if the value of a work cannot have the aspect of endurance as well as mutability.[9] She speaks of evaluation as a purely subjective affair, a function of the personal economy of the evaluator, never entertaining the reality that a group, a culture can agree on an enduring evaluation.

Reader-centered criticism, of which Smith's view is an expression, weakens the discipline of reading to the extent that it does not recognize the demands that the work makes. The belief in the objectivity of a text does not necessarily entail an *ideal* reader, but it presupposes a reader that is adequate to the text. In transferring authority from the author or the work to the reader, the reader sets his own standards for adequacy.

It doesn't follow from the variability of readers' responses to classic works (or, for that matter, works of any kind) that the works are empty of intrinsic value, or that their value is a matter of pure contingency. In reviewing responses to a classic, one finds common ground as well as differences. Nor does it follow from the variety of responses that they are mutually exclusive. We read the criticism of others not only to quarrel with it, but also to enhance our understanding and appreciation of a work. Indeed, the power of a work can be measured by the variety of intelligent and perceptive responses it provokes. We don't need to be in full agreement with a reading to appreciate the adequacy of a response to a work. "Interesting," we respond, meaning that we want the time to entertain the response and perhaps admit it to our own personal understanding. However different the responses, what the reader must discover in a classic is something that appeals to our common humanity. Harold Bloom writes: "All that the Western Canon can bring one is the proper use of one's solitude, that solitude whose final form is confrontation with one's own mortality."[10] The Western Canon may bring us other things as well, but Bloom's response is of the kind that our classics require.

I give a course in the modern short novel (each one a classic) that in virtually every text challenges both the assumptions and the comforts of the students. Some of the works are Tolstoy's *The Death of Ivan Ilych*, Conrad's *Heart of Darkness* and *The Secret Sharer*, James's *The Beast in the Jungle*, Dostoevsky's *Notes from Underground*, and Kafka's *The Metamorphosis*. *The Death of Ivan Ilyich* is the story of a typical man of the rising upper middle class in Czarist Russia, apparently successful in marriage and career (he rises to prominence as a judge), who becomes mortally ill as the result of a fall from a stepladder while decorating his home. The accident, and his subsequent illness and suffering turn into a judgment of the life he leads. As he lies dying, he comes to see the utter emptiness of his life. Tolstoy's language has the transparency of a prosecution, and even the least sophisticated reader has access to the painful reality of Ivan Ilych's existence. We are told that "Ivan Ilych's life was the most ordinary, the most simple and therefore the most terrible." A friend of mine taught the story a number of years ago and an engineering student in his class went up to him after the discussion clearly distressed. He experienced the story as an assault on his deepest desires and ambitions. Ivan Ilych's life before his fall was the life he wanted for himself, and in the school in which he was being prepared for that life he was being taught it was empty of meaning.

The student had a shock of recognition, but of the kind that attacked rather than confirmed his convictions. His distress was an implicit acknowledgment of the power of the story. It is doubtful that it changed his career plans, but it produced a kind of disturbance. (Was it fortuitous that my friend had this experience as a student? Years before as an undergraduate, destined to follow in his father's footsteps into the medical profession, he rose from a reading of *Anna Karenina* and mortified his father by deciding to become a student of literature.) I myself have never had such a vivid experience of teaching *The Death of Ivan Ilych,* but when I tell the students that the story may be *their* story, they begin to experience the power and the challenge of the work. The challenge can be met with an acceptance of the judgment that the story passes on its characters and by implication on every one of its readers. Or it can be resisted. Tolstoy's intense and idiosyncratic spirituality devalues ordinary life, attributes to it a squalor that a sensitive and intelligent reader need not share. But it is a mark of the reader's intelligence and sensitivity that he or she be alive to the challenge.

Part of Tolstoy's indictment of Ivan Ilych concerns his performance as a judge. His disinterestedness and objectivity are viewed as signs of coldness. But, as a note to an edition of the tale makes clear, Ivan Ilych as judge exemplifies the judicial reform that occurred under the liberal regime of Alexander II in which a new code of justice was established in 1864, making its administration more rational and equitable. Tolstoy's judgment reflects an old feudal bias that licenses the passions even in the administration of justice. Ivan Ilych is a Russian judge from the upper middle class, administering justice after the liberation of the serfs and the installation of a new legal code, which introduces equality before the law. It is an issue in our reading of the story that Ivan Ilych's dispassionate administration of justice becomes part of the evidence that he lacks "the sap of life." I remark this moment not to endorse a politically correct reading of *The Death of Ivan Ilych* but simply to assert that a classic does not have to be swallowed whole. An admiring reader can judge this moment in the story as representing a class bias he does not share. The bias shows itself in Ivan Ilych's idealization of the peasant Gerasim as the repository of natural piety. Tolstoy's aristocratic affinity for the peasant does not qualify as universal experience. The classic does and does not exist in a timeless space. Its universality rises out of and is inflected and refracted by local experience and national or class bias. Timelessness and historicity are both aspects of the classic. Presentmindedness is an unavoidable response of the reader, who may not share Tolstoy's intense "Christian" conviction that ordinary life is all squalor.

In the course, every work that follows *The Death of Ivan Ilych* offers a comparable challenge. How can the student reconcile himself to the vitality of Dostoevsky's perverse and often obnoxious underground man? And there are comparable struggles, marked by accommodation and resistance, in responding (with Marlow) to Kurtz's heroic nihilism, to the unnamed captain of *The Secret Sharer* who embraces a murderer in the process of achieving self-mastery and authority, or to Camus's stranger whose murderous amoralism becomes a path to self-discovery and joy in being alive. Difficulty, paradox, challenge: They characterize all the works on my list. And to the extent that the students glimpse the difficulty, engage it (the authority of the teacher must create the opportunity for engagement, not enforce a particular reading), they have experienced the power of the classic. Wanting to be open to the work, to listen to what it has to say and teach and to the pleasure it affords does not necessarily translate into piety. Piety involves the suspension of the critical faculty and so long as susceptible readers maintain their capacity to interpret, resist, and evaluate, they are not in a pious relation to the text. The admiration of a work must be the result of an experience of it, not of a prescriptive assertion that a work is great, but that experience cannot come about if the reader is not open to the voice or voices of the work.


## II


In *Great Books: My Adventures with Homer, Rousseau, Woolf and Other Indestructible Writers of the Western World,* David Denby provides a lively account of what goes on in the classrooms where the classics are still taught. A forty-eight-year-old film critic for *New York Magazine*, Denby decided to return for a year to his alma mater Columbia College to reexperience the Great Books that he had read more than two decades before as an undergraduate. The return was motivated partly by his "reading with increasing amazement, the debate about the nature of higher education" in America ("Should groups formerly without much power—women, as well as minorities—be asked to read through a curriculum dominated by works written by Dead White European Males?")[11] and partly by a sense of his own cultural impoverishment as a consumer of popular culture, estranged from the experience of serious reading. "By the early nineties I was beginning to be sick at heart, sick not of movies or of movie criticism but of living my life inside what the French philosopher Guy Debord has called 'the society of the spectacle'—the immense system of representations and simulacra, the thick atmosphere of information and imagery and attitudes that forms the mental condition and habits of almost any adult living in a media society in the late twentieth century"(15).

Denby enters the classroom in a double role, as participant and observer. He is separated from the other students by age and experience. He will be rereading the Great Books as an antidote to the dissatisfaction he experiences with the popular culture that provides his younger classmates with *their* satisfactions. They will resist what he desires. Not entirely, for like the eighteen year olds in his class, Denby is a modern person capable of being provoked and offended by archaic attitudes and ideas, like the acceptance of slavery in Aristotle or the hostility to democracy in Plato.

One difference between Denby's earlier experience of the Great Books and his present experience is what he perceives to be the current indifference or outright hostility of many students to the Great Books. Popular culture and multicultural ideology acquired before entry into college provide the resistance. Denby reports an extracurricular meeting between a professor and students unhappy about the Western orientation of the curriculum. The complaints are predictable: "The underlying message of C.C. [Contemporary Civilization] and Lit Hum . . . is that in these books, the culture of these white men is supreme." "You let women and people of color into the school, but the books in the core courses are all white." "Why did I have to listen in Music Humanities to this Mozart? . . . Why is Mozart better than some African drummer? There are all kinds of beautiful music I see excluded from Music Humanities. There are no women, no people of color"(89).

In *Textual Power* Robert Scholes in effect makes the case for the complaining students. He argues that "a major function of the teacher of fiction should be to help students identify their own collectivities, their group or class interests, by means of the representation of typical figures and situations in fictional texts." He goes on to say:

. . . instead of subordinating their human, ethical, and political reactions to some ideal of literary value—pardoning Paul Claudel for "writing well" as modernism [Auden, not modernism] would have it—our students should learn finally how to criticize Paul Claudel, or anyone else, from some viewpoint beyond the merely personal—and the merely literary.
    . . . My point here is that criticism is always made on behalf of a group. Even "taste" is never a truly personal thing but a carefully inculcated norm, usually established by a powerful social class. . . .[12]

Scholes opposes the human, ethical, and political to the "merely" literary and personal, and he conflates the human and ethical with group identity. Students, he argues, must be helped in identifying "their own collectivities, their group or class interests." But, one might reasonably ask: Can teachers be expected to know better than the students and their families what those interests are? Each teacher would have to inform himself about the identities of Jews, African Americans, Native Americans, Asians, white Anglo-Saxons, and so on, to understand the group interests of his students. And to understand those identities and interests, he might have to sort out the differences between secular and orthodox Jews, Ashkenazi and Central European Jews, Koreans and Chinese, Vietnamese and Cambodians, Mexicans and Puerto Ricans, Apaches and Iroquois, black males and black females, white males and white females—there is no end. And even if that were possible, what can the teacher possibly know of all the variations in the students' experiences of their group identity or, more accurately, of the multiplicity of their group identities? (What would he make of a young woman whose father is African American and mother Jewish?) And what if a student doesn't want her "group identity" to figure in her education? There is the patronizing assumption that students want or require this kind of help. Which is not to say that ethnic or racial or religious identity might not play itself out in the classroom. I would think that its most interesting expressions would come not from a programmatic attempt to teach identity, but from spontaneous and unpredictable responses of the students.

Scholes is a learned and perceptive literary theorist, who in his work displays an admirable independent-mindedness. So it comes as something of shock in reading *Textual Power* to find him speaking of criticism as "always made on behalf of a group," and of taste as "never a truly personal thing but a carefully inculcated norm usually established by a powerful class." Scholes seems to be saying two different, perhaps contradictory, things: Criticism reflects a group judgment, whether social or ethnic or racial, and taste is the internalization of the values of the dominant class. What is consistent in the passage, however, is the idea of taste and evaluative criticism as products of group-think. How would Scholes then account for differences in taste between members of the same group? In a later chapter Scholes presents a sophisticated critique of Stanley Fish's idea of a literary community, which oddly enough would seem to have an affinity with Scholes's conception of the socially constructed character of taste and literary judgment. (Isn't Scholes affirming the personal response when he writes, contra Fish, "When Wittgenstein said that our world is bounded by our language he did not say that we had no [personal] freedom within the boundaries. If you play chess you can only do certain things with the pieces—or you will no longer be playing chess. Those constraints in themselves never tell you what move to make."[13]) You can acknowledge the social and historical influences on the formation of taste and judgment without denying the personal character of judgment. Scholes says that he wants to "open the way between the literary and verbal text and the social text in which we live."[14] His target is the self-referential aestheticism of the New Criticism or a certain version of it. However, it is one thing to make a path between literature and society; it is another thing to *reduce* the literary to the social in whatever form: racial, ethnic, class, or gendered. The complaining students at Columbia and elsewhere have their allies in the faculties of universities.

The antagonism toward the Great Books willy-nilly becomes part of the experience of the courses in a way that it never was when David Denby took the courses in the mid-60s or when I took them in the early 50s. Denby describes the teaching of several professors, among them Edward Taylor and Anders Stephanson, who present an interesting contrast in pedagogical approach. Professor Taylor says: "These books will form you"(43). There is an authoritative assumption in this statement, not widely shared, that the students are unformed and receptive to formation by the texts. Taylor's ambition for his course is in the spirit of the ancient Greeks, for whom education was *paideia,* a forming of the self. Perhaps it would be closer to the truth to speak of the students as already formed in ways that these books will challenge. Education is *re*formation. Professor Taylor's style is to challenge the student to experience the power of *The Iliad,* for example, through a formal approach—that is, by showing how it is put together. Denby understands this approach as "a defense against banality. . . . [B]y deconstructing it or appropriating it to some modern perception of class, power, gender—none of which applied to Homer—you made the poem meaningless. The older classics, Taylor implied, would not live if the books were turned into a mere inadequate version of the present"(45–46). Rather than impose an interpretation, he wants to elicit his own understanding from the students (perhaps a subtler form of imposition). The method is sometimes called Socratic. Taylor doesn't just tell the students what he wants, of course. "Imploring and urging, he pulled it out of them, asking leading questions, dropping hints, asking them to read aloud passages that have no apparent connection, passages spaced far apart in the book. At times, the class stalled, and he retreated from his point, literally stepping backward and letting his head drop for a moment before approaching from another angle, like a guerilla force making tentative forays in the jungle. Eventually, he would coax them out of hiding and surround them"(43–44).

Taylor's approach contrasts with that of Professor Anders Stephanson, who announces to his class: "One never accepts the texts as they seem to be. . . . One always interrogates them"(43). The difference is clear. Taylor challenges the students to be adequate to the classics, Stephanson challenges the texts to reveal their political motives, which are less than benign. It would appear that Taylor is the authoritarian imposing the text on the students, whereas Stephanson is the empowerer of the students in their resistance to the texts. Appearances are deceiving, for there is *at least* as much pedagogical authoritarianism in Stephanson's doctrinal assertion, *"Your most everyday assumptions are arbitrary—politically determined,"* as there is in the claim made for the classics. Is it not an exercise in authority for a teacher to assert: "That the books had survived for so long was proof not of their universality but of exactly the opposite—that they were part of a tradition that had triumphed politically"(42)? Interrogation in practice is a kind of inquisition in which the text is brought before a tribunal of politically committed interrogators. Authority does not disappear; rather, it is transferred to the professorial interrogator who manages the responses of the students. The approach offers little opportunity for the student to resist this view. Reading becomes a demystification of the sophistications of the text and the innocent delusions of the student reader. Only the professor is knowing, capable of the right kind of interrogation.

Denby doesn't say it, but Professor Stephanson's approach can easily lead to the banality that Taylor is trying to resist: the deconstruction of *The Iliad,* for example, "to some modern perception of class, power, gender"(46). For Stephanson relevance becomes a standard for judging how a classic satisfies or fails to satisfy some contemporary understandings. For Taylor, relevance defines the ways in which a text works to educate, that is, to shape or modify understanding and the self. Taylor gets away with it, because of his gifts as a teacher. But this authoritative pedagogy has become disreputable. The preferred style is Stephanson's style of "interrogation," where the authority of the professor is masked. The intended effect of Stephanson's approach on the students is to create a political disposition toward the texts. The intended effect of Taylor's approach is subtler and harder to measure. How can we know that the classic is forming or reforming a student? What would be the signs? Most teaching is received in silence, and it is only the rare student who will speak or write with the eloquence of discovery and self-discovery. Which is not to say that things are not happening to students in the silence of listening. What is happening may become evident only years later and in retrospect.

Taylor is a distinguished example of a tradition in which the teacher openly asserts his authority and becomes as it were a medium of the work for the students. It may not be fashionable, but a gifted teacher can make such teaching a memorable experience. Stephanson exemplifies the politically motivated skepticism toward the classics that characterizes much of the profession today. Both kinds of teaching assume the authority of the teacher; Stephanson's approach challenges the authority of the text. He encounters the text and its ideology with his own ideology. What if the student doesn't share his teacher's ideology once he has become familiar with it? It marks him as mystified. A failure in Taylor's students to grasp the formalism of a classic text reflects a lack of sophistication. "Mystification" is a political judgment, "lack of sophistication" a pedagogical one.

In the debate about authority or "advocacy in the classroom" (the title of a recent anthology of essays), there are those who say that advocacy is inimical to disinterested inquiry and those who believe that it is inescapable. And there are those who resist the debate, because the meaning of advocacy is unclear. Clearly (or at least it seems to be clear to me), intellectual neutrality in a classroom is undesirable, if not impossible. We all remember our passionate teachers who had views on subjects. When is the strongly expressed view or advocacy appropriate in the classroom?

There is the matter of relevancy of the advocacy to the subject matter at hand. Louis Menand offers an obvious example: A math professor "spends his time lecturing about why we should all emulate the moral life of the Victorians but fails to demonstrate any connection between this idea and the subject matter of mathematics."[15] This is an easy, indeed too easy, example. Almost everyone would agree about the inappropriate behavior of the math professor. It is not an example of the crux of the debate. Menand offers another example, which is closer to the heart of the matter: "[A] professor knows that, say, *Heart of Darkness* is not a racist text but teaches it as if it were a racist text because she believes that students should be impressed with the need to combat racism." As I say, closer to the heart of the matter, but not close enough. There is something askew about the example, for it suggests a cognitive dissonance in the professor that is hardly typical. The problem arises when a professor believes a text (*Heart of Darkness* is an excellent example) to be racist or, for that matter, antiracist, and then advocates the view in a way that prevents the students from considering other views. This is indoctrination, not teaching.

Does this mean that a professor is to abdicate authority and not assert his views strongly? What is required here is a kind of pedagogical tact, for which there are no formulas. The strength of the professor's views should lie in the compelling nature of the argument (its logic and evidence) that he brings to bear, not in his tone or insistence. The presentation of the view should provide an opening for questions, challenges, resistance. It is, of course, true that the professor generally has the advantage of a more experienced command of argument, and so he must qualify his authority by a willingness to hear in the less articulate formulations of students a truth that may contradict his or her own sense of the truth. The issue then is not whether advocacy is desirable, but how the professor deploys authority in the classroom. An authority openly displayed and modestly exercised is, in my view, superior to an authority that conceals itself under the pretense of the "openness" of an interrogation that is driven by an ideological agenda.

In the late 1960s and early 1970s, the authority of the teacher was under constant challenge. Those of us who taught in the fraught conditions of the time have stories to tell. Here is one such story. I taught D. H. Lawrence's *Women in Love* to a class at MIT absorbed by the countercultural passions of the time. There were students with strong political commitments against the war in Vietnam and for civil rights. There were also students devoted to self-fulfillment, or doing your own thing. There were "touchy-feely" encounter groups, avatars of the new-age "lifestyles" that were coming into being. All this is necessary background to my experience in teaching the novel. At one point in the discussion a male student lifted the pile of books and dropped them loudly on his desk, visibly disgusted with the discussion. (Acting out was a fairly common phenomenon.) In the tolerant spirit of the time (the tolerance of teachers for the behavior of the students, not the reverse), I asked the student in the mildest of tones: "What's the matter?" His answer: "Why all this cerebral talk about a book that's passionate and gets you in the gut?" I responded with all the professorial dignity at my command. "I know how to talk about the narrative form of the novel, its themes and language, but I'm not sure what one can say about the gut. What do you suggest?" A somewhat pompous reply. But the challenge to the student was fair game. Students were questioning and challenging professional authority. Why not give him a crack at taking charge? But he would have none of it. "Why ask me, you're the teacher?" So authority was still alive and well. But in engaging him, I had clearly put myself at a disadvantage. I could see from the expressions on the faces of the students who were observing the contest with a certain fascination that I had not risen to the occasion. A sudden inspiration. We had been talking about the wrestling scene between Rupert Birkin and Gerald Crich in which they strip themselves naked and achieve male bonding. "Ah, I know what you want: the rest of the class should leave, you and I strip naked and wrestle." "Yeah!" Laughter in the class. "Forget about it," I said, with a sense of satisfaction that I had finally risen to the occasion.

The student was indifferent to the difficulty of the work. He did not want to have to struggle to understand what was complex and recalcitrant in it. He looked to reading for instant gratification, and if it was not forthcoming it had nothing to say to him—or the teacher who tried to express the difficulty had nothing to say to him. There was nothing eccentric about his response; it was the going fashion in the academy. In the 1960s, it was the professor who was challenged, now it is the student who is invited by the professor to join with him or her in challenging the text.

The students are only fitfully present in Denby's book. Its interest lies mainly in his account of the ways of teaching the Great Books and his rediscovery of them. The students appear most vividly in their resistance to the work. Denby also shows them in their indifference and on occasion in their warming to a teacher's exposition. They do not share in the excitement of Denby's discoveries (or rediscoveries). How could a student in his eighteenth year be expected to have the following response to *The Odyssey*?

The gigantic poem is built around an excruciating paradox: the temptation to rest, to fill your stomach is almost overwhelming, yet the instant you rest, you are in danger of losing consciousness or life itself. In the end, short of death or oblivion, there is not rest, a state of being that might be called the Western glory and the Western disease. That Homer cannot attain—that there's something demonic, unappeasable, and unreachably alien in the spirit of the *Odyssey* as well as in *The Iliad*—has not much figured in the epic's popular reputation as a hearty adventure saga. It was a finer, more exhilarating and challenging work than most people thought. (81)

One might imagine Denby as an inarticulate student in the 1960s. Inarticulateness in the presence of the classics (a fumbling speech) is a condition of most students, however intelligent. They are not yet sufficiently formed by experience to encounter the classics with the mixture of responsiveness and critical skepticism that the classics demand. Denby's interesting responses would not have occurred if he had not had an initial encounter, and had not experienced the world and matured in the interval. Though Denby speaks of his dissatisfaction with the media world in which he lives and writes, *Great Books* does not represent his farewell to that world. He remains in it, but impressively apart from it in the way he experiences the classics. "The courses in the Western classics force us to ask all those questions about self and society we no longer address without embarrassment—the questions our media-trained habits of irony have tricked us out of asking. In order to ask those questions, students need to be enchanted before they are disenchanted. They need to love the text before they attack the subtext . . . they need a chance at making a self before they are told that it doesn't exist"(463). Professor Taylor urges his students "to think double." Denby's book is an illustration and realization of that possibility. What makes the book a salutary event is that it is the work of an unrepentant media critic who makes a case for high culture. He accepts in his own life an unresolved tension between the claims of high culture and of popular culture.

Denby's book and the Columbia curriculum have been severely attacked by Helen Vendler on aesthetic grounds. "[Denby has imbibed] Columbia's tendency with literary texts, which is to fasten on the political and moral over the erotic or esthetic or epistemological; and such an emphasis is a standing invitation to correctness or incorrectness, since it steers discussion, willy-nilly, toward currently agitated, political and moral questions."[16] She cites the example of *Heart of Darkness* in which Denby resists the view that Conrad's story "endorses the colonial ambitions of the British Empire." Both sides of the debate (*Heart of Darkness* as imperialist in its imagination or as anticolonial in its sentiment) would be in Vendler's view irrelevant to the aesthetic achievement of the novel. She is certainly right to reject the kind of criticism (criticism is hardly the word for it) that turns a work into an occasion for a political debate, serving a contemporary agenda. But she impoverishes literature in setting the political and the moral over against the erotic, the aesthetic, and the epistemological. (Why, one wonders, do the aesthetic, and the epistemological belong on one side of the opposition?) *Heart of Darkness* has an important and inescapable political content. The question is how one should read it. To say that it be approached aesthetically is either vacuous or dangerous: vacuous if it means that we simply attend to the narrative construction of the tale, the ordering of events and to the language employed, and we have nothing to say about what it signifies; dangerous if we address the charismatic presence of Kurtz without understanding it morally and politically. In doing so, we would be complicit with what Primo Levi calls "the lechery of aestheticism."

In reading *Heart of Darkness* or any work with a political or moral content (and there is hardly a work without a moral content), we, of course, need to understand how the content is mediated by genre. *Heart of Darkness* is not a political speech or a sermon. We should not commit the error, in Vendler's scornful words, of "treating fictions as moral pep-pills or moral emetics" and ignore "the complex psychological and formal motives of a work of art." But it is an impoverishment of literature to reduce the moral to its therapeutic or cathartic function, as Vendler does. Henry James, whose aesthetic sensibility was the equal of that of any writer, knew with the authority of an imaginative writer and a critic that the imagination was inescapably moral, and that the formalities of art, its psychological complexity, were inextricably entwined with the moral. Denby is not one of our distinguished critics, but his book is an admirable attempt to understand and resist the ideological challenges to literary study. In simply preferring art to morality, the private to the public, Vendler fails to meet those challenges. The effect of her aestheticism is to cede the field to the ideologues, for she offers no advice about how we are to read the moral and political content of literature.

In his well-known essay, "On the Teaching of Modern Literature"(1961), Lionel Trilling describes his disappointment with the responses of his students to the classics of modern literature. He found that his students did not offer the expected resistance to *Notes from Underground, Heart of Darkness,* and other works on his syllabus. "I asked them to look into the Abyss," Trilling writes, "and, both dutifully and gladly, they have looked into the Abyss, and the Abyss has greeted them with the grave courtesy of all serious objects of study, saying: 'Interesting, am I not? And *exciting,* if you consider how deep I am and what dread beasts lie at my bottom. Have it well in mind that a knowledge of me contributes materially to your being whole, or well-rounded men.'"[17] The students were not threatened by the Abyss, because it had become a familiar notion. They responded not to the vivid representation of it in the works they read, but to the cultural talk it had become. Trilling found that he had to cope with a sophistication, a false sophistication that screened the students from the resistant power of the work. His essay may not describe the responses of students today (the Abyss has virtually disappeared from view), but it represents in a general way the challenge that faces the teacher (should face the teacher, in my view) every time he or she enters the classroom: how to remove the screens that prevent students from experiencing the power, the sometimes threatening power, of a work of art.

### III

Does critical theory help or hinder the appreciation and understanding of a work of art? It depends on what one means by theory. Gerald Graff provides a useful definition of the usefulness of theory in practical criticism:

"[L]iterary theory is a discourse concerned with the legitimating principles, assumptions, and premises of literature and literary criticism. Contrary to the stipulation of recent pragmatist arguments against theory, literary theory may but need not be a system of foundational discourse that aims to "govern" critical practice from some outside metaphysical standpoint. When literary theory is attacked, this systematic or foundational conception of theory is usually the target, whether the opponents be disgruntled humanists, deconstructionists or pragmatists. But it is at least as legitimate, and more in line with normal usage, to think of literary theory not as a set of systematic principles, necessarily, or a founding philosophy, but simply as an inquiry into assumptions, premises, and legitimating principles and concepts.[18]

Certainly in discussing the interpretation of a work, one might have to reflect upon assumptions of an interpretation, especially when it conflicts with another interpretation. At one point in a class discussion of Henry James's *The Beast in the Jungle,* I introduced Eve Sedgwick's provocative interpretation in which she makes the hero John Marcher out to be suffering from homosexual panic. The "secret" that the story discloses is his incapacity to love a woman. The story does not disclose the cause of the incapacity (one might say it is not interested to do so). Sedgwick, however, is provoked in her reading to speculate about the cause. And the evidence, it would seem, is there in the final encounter with the man whose face is "scarred with passion," bereaved over the loss of a loved one, and in the language earlier in the story ("queerness," "gaiety," and "perversion"). Sedgwick makes much of the fact that Marcher is aroused to knowledge about his incapacity for love not in the loss of his companion, May Bartram, whose love he cannot reciprocate, but in his encounter with the man.[19]

The class resisted the interpretation, because the homosexual theme is not expressed in the story. If Sedgwick is right, then the truth remains a secret not only from Marcher, but from James as well. How could this be? Here it was necessary for me to explain the conditions under which such an interpretation was plausible—not the same thing as persuading the students to accept the interpretation. What Sedgwick's reading assumes is that the writer may not fully understand the story he is telling. D. H. Lawrence, with a writer's knowledge of his own ignorance, said, "Never trust the artist. Trust the tale." Something in a story might invite a psychoanalytic reading which penetrates to a level beneath the writer's conscious intention. Such a view gives license to a reading such as Sedgwick's, though it does not guarantee the persuasiveness of the reading. Another possibility is that a writer may know what is unexpressed in the story and choose indirection and implication to express it, because of some taboo or self-imposed censorship. In either case, Sedgwick's interpretation is an instance of the need to reflect on the assumptions of one's interpretation.

Graff's sensible view of the uses of theory does not correspond to normal practice in the profession, despite his claim that it does. Theories tend to govern interpretation, rather than simply reflect on its assumptions. Even Graff betrays an affinity for systematic theory when, in lamenting the fact that theory "has become accepted as a useful option for graduate students and advanced undergraduates," he speaks of the division of spoils between theory and tradition (does he mean practical criticism?) as "prevent[ing] the theoretical impulse from exerting a coordinating role and divert[ing] it toward its own brand of isolationism."[20]

What happens to a classic when contemporary critical theory scrutinizes it? I will take as an example an edition of Dickens's *Great Expectations*, a part of a series of editions for undergraduate courses that present the texts, followed by essays illustrative of the prevailing theoretical perspectives in literary studies: deconstruction, feminist criticism, gender criticism, cultural criticism, psychoanalytic criticism, and in certain instances, Marxist criticism. The edition contains a critical history of the work. Each essay is preceded by a general introduction to the approach.

The critical history reads as if it were the prehistory to the more substantial achievement of contemporary approaches. It rehearses a variety of interpretations up to the advent of critical theory to show how they "assume unproblematically the organic unity of the work and the possibility of true selfhood . . . . Most readings of *Great Expectations* through the 1980's affirm the universal humanistic ideals of love, charity and fellow feeling as the value of the integrated individual who can learn to put those ideals into practice."[21] Who affirms these ideals, the reader or the novel? The statement is unclear. Whoever the affirmer may be there is the suggestion of something deplorably naive in the affirmation. In contrast, critical theory (feminist, deconstructive, New Historicist) will "question the ability of a text, any text to serve as an unproblematic repository of human values." As David Bromwich remarks, "[h]istory [according to the critical theorists] can be divided into two parts: first, the way they used to do things, . . . and second, the way we do things now. . . ."[22] The critical history that the editor of the volume passes on to unwitting undergraduates is nothing short of a travesty. It simply ignores its complexity. Anyone who lived through the history, as I have, remembers a criticism in which there were quarrels about interpretation, sensitivity to ambiguities and paradoxes in the texts, and the willingness of critics to criticize as well as praise. Piety before the organically unified work in the past is the self-aggrandizing myth of the critical theorist. Critics of American literature took seriously Lawrence's injunction never to trust the artist, an anticipation of the deconstructionist claim that the text does not know itself. (There is a difference between saying that the text may not know itself and saying that it may never know itself.) It is true that the organic metaphor informed pre-critical theory criticism, but it hardly encompassed its activity.

Critical theory is distinguished from the criticism of the past in the pride with which it declares its systematic (I am tempted to say indiscriminate) resistance to texts. "Theory renders possible, sometimes even seems to require, readings of literary texts that resist, contradict, or invalidate the terms, assumptions, and implications that the texts themselves seem to authorize"(456). The possibility of resisting, contradicting, invalidating becomes a practice even when the text does not require it. It is the practice of deconstruction, which had a brief run as the dominant critical theory. Though it gave way to other theories (feminism, New Historicism, psychoanalysis, Marxism), deconstruction has survived in sublimated form in these theories. It could not maintain its privileged position in literary study as an end itself, because it had no other motive than discovering and eliciting the incoherences of a text. This may provide a nihilistic pleasure, but it doesn't satisfy political, moral, and aesthetic interests that persist in our reading as well as our living. Deconstruction has become a means of questioning texts and institutions from various perspectives but not an end in itself. The New Historicist, the feminist, the gender critic, the critic interested in questions of ethnicity all use deconstruction; they resist being *used* by it—that is, being undone by it. An endless deconstruction might deconstruct the assumptions of New Historicism and feminism and indeed of every ideological agenda. What the various critical theories have in common, however, is a deconstructive animus against humanistic assumptions of the wholeness and autonomy of works of literature. Critical theory views texts as "self-contradictory productions of cultural and economic forces [beyond] personal control"(458), though, interestingly enough, it exempts itself from the conditions of self-contradiction and incoherence when it states its aim as "reveal[ing] to students that good criticism is informed by a set of coherent assumptions"(vi). (One might ask, if the critics' assumptions can be coherent, why not those of the text it "interrogates"?)

"Theory," Gerald Graff remarks, "is what inevitably arises when literary conventions and critical definitions once taken for granted have become objects of generalized discussion and dispute."[23] In other words, it is born in intellectual crisis, and it follows from this view of its origins that when the dust settles and certain agreements and understandings are reached, it would disappear or recede in the background and a routinized practical criticism would take over. Such criticism would be "theorized," that is, it would apply a theoretical perspective to a text without critically reflecting on the assumptions of the theory. As "generalized discussion," theory challenges prevailing views. When, however, it takes a positive turn, a way of understanding literature with its own definitions and understanding of literary conventions, it becomes a practice in which it takes things for granted, for example, the idea that the text is generically incoherent or that it conceals motives of domination. It then doesn't so much challenge accepted ways of understanding as it challenges in increasingly predictable ways the texts' self-understandings, becoming as routinized as any untheoretical practical criticism. No deconstruction I know turns on its own assumptions to question whether all texts are incoherent; no New Historicist entertains the possibility that a work of literature can transcend its time, that is, the conventional understandings of the historical period in which it is written; no Marxist critic can resist the desire to find class conflict as the motive force of a narrative. What I want to contest is the self-congratulation of critical theorists who pride themselves as radical probers of established ways of knowing.

Readings of *Great Expectations* before the advent of critical theory, if they had any interest, did considerably more than affirm humanistic ideals, though they expressed what is hard to dispute: that love, charity, and fellow feeling is what Pip claims to have achieved in his telling of his story. A critic of the pretheoretical past might not have recognized the novel as a reflection "of the kind of modern social and political power that Foucault found epitomized in Bentham's panopticon, a model for a prison in which isolated inmates are always subject to the possibility of surveillance" and conclude from it that "Pip's autobiography is a form of inevitable 'self-oppression' rather than 'liberating self-expression'"(459). With the hindsight of what he has learned, Pip narrates his fears and guilt, his "mortal terror" of others and himself as he is growing up. "I was in mortal terror of my interlocutor with the ironed leg; I was in mortal terror of myself, from whom an awful promise had been extracted; I had no hope of deliverance through my all-powerful sister who repulsed me at every turn; I am afraid to think of what I might have done, on requirement, in the secrecy of my terror"(34). He has reason to fear his hostile environment (all the adult characters in his life, with the exception of Joe Gargery, are menacing figures) and he has reason to fear his own capacity for violence when he identifies himself with George Barnwell, the murderer of his uncle, while listening to Wopsle's account of *The Tragedy of George Barnwell*, and with the attacker of his sister. "With my head full of George Barnwell, I was at first disposed to believe that *I* must have had some hand in the attack upon my sister, or at all events that as her near relation, popularly known to be under obligations to her, I was a more legitimate object of suspicion than anyone else"(125). If this is what counts as "self-oppression," it was already understood in the "pretheoretical" or "humanist" criticism of Robert Garis, who represents Orlick, the attacker of Pip's sister, as Pip's alter ego. Why this makes the autobiography a "form of self-oppression" is not at all clear. What is clear is that the novel is being made to serve a particular ideological agenda about texts and institutions: All claims to freedom are illusory.

No critic who writes with authority is a merely passive register of a text. He inevitably appropriates it to his own interests. The issue is whether the appropriation contributes to an appreciation of what the work is about. When Edward Said approaches *Great Expectations* with a desire to find a colonialist theme, he focuses on events in the novel that have largely gone unremarked, but are undeniably present in the novel. The ex-convict Abel Magwitch, Pip's benefactor, illegally returns from Australia, the traditional dumping ground for Britain's criminals. For Said, the return of Magwitch and his demise are an emblem of Britain's imperial view that criminals, incapable of redemption, are doomed to be "permanent outsiders." Since Australia in the nineteenth-century British mind is identified with criminality, Pip becomes "a hardworking trader in the East, where Britain's other colonies offer a sort of normality that Australia never could"(526). An event in the novel is contextualized in the drama of British imperialism that is Said's subject. Is there anything wrong with such a reading? Does it advance our knowledge of the novel? Not as a novel, I would argue. Said has captured a moment in British imperial history as it is represented in *Great Expectations,* but how does this moment contribute to our understanding of Pip's ambition to become a gentlemen, to the falsity of that ambition, and to the awakening of his capacity to love? Said does not say that Pip's new profession as a trader compromises his moral development. He in fact makes no connection between them. The colonialist theme stands apart. Said apparently feels no obligation to reconcile it, because the text is no longer a coherent whole, no longer the sum of its parts.

Criticism, inspired by postmodern theory, sees the texts as fragments with each theoretical perspective specializing in one or another set of fragments. The justification for such a view is, of course, the assumption that the work does not possess organic unity. It is not theory that dissolves it into fragments, the critical theorist argues, but the work itself that is in fragments. The evidence of incoherence and contradiction in a work does not prove such a view, though it may give it plausibility. What it fails to acknowledge are consistencies of pattern that represent an imaginative effort to achieve coherence and meaning, to pull the whole thing together. In practice, all interpretations, including those driven by critical theory, look for consistencies, otherwise intelligible interpretation would be impossible. The coherence of the discourse substitutes for the coherence of the text.

Integrity is another word for coherence. Critical theory challenges the integrity of the text and its relative autonomy, eroding the boundaries between text and context, so that critics of whatever theoretical persuasion (New Historicism, deconstruction, psychoanalysis, gender study) can extract items from a work and assimilate them to the particular discourses that interest them. For instance, the recurrent appearance of hands in *Great Expectations* becomes a trope for a particular Victorian obsession:

The placement of hand on genitals remains a secret in the Victorian novel, but like all secrets it wants to be told. . . .

Why hands? An account of their place in Victorian culture would consider
the wealth of its tracts on chirology, palmistry, and graphology. The fact is not
simply that the hand was paid a great deal of attention, but that—given the extent of Victorian self-regulation, both literary and sartorial—it was one of the few
anatomical parts regularly available for attention: the usual costume of middle-
class English adults in the nineteenth century covered all of the body but the
head and the hands. (575)

"Hands" have migrated from the novel to discourses about chirology,
palmistry, and graphology.

There is a particular unintended irony in the way the image of the
hand is deployed—I am tempted to say fetishized—in this essay (in
"gender criticism"). "Hands" is an important theme in *Hard Times*, a
novel Dickens wrote shortly before *Great Expectations*. In the novel,
Dickens attacks the industrial system much in the way that Ruskin attacked it a little later in "The Nature of the Gothic," for its fragmentation of the person. Factory operatives have become hands, in effect losing
their integrity as persons. In a sense, the critic who focuses on hands in
*Great Expectations*, losing sight of the novel as a whole, replicates the dis-
integrative effect that Dickens criticizes in *Hard Times*. It is an instruc-
tive irony, for it dramatizes the cross-purposes of novelist and reader.
Dickens does not simply affirm wholeness, he criticizes its absence in the
lives of the characters who inhabit the world he represents. The critic resists the basis of such a view (to be sure, in a novel in which the terms of
whole and part have a different meaning) on behalf of a critical doctrine
that disparages the very idea of wholeness. *Great Expectations* becomes
subject to a division of labor in which critics representing various theoretical discourses appropriate its various parts to their discursive systems.

Gerald Graff's proposal that we "teach the conflicts," that is, the theoretical conflicts about what constitutes the text and its meanings, may
be a way into literature for those who have no initial love for it. The Bedford edition of *Great Expectations* is in the spirit of Graff's proposal,
though in fairness to Graff's proposal, the edition in contrast stacks the
cards in favor of one side of the conflict. The "humanist" past (a term that
covers a heterogeneity) is summarized condescendingly as a naive pre-
lude to the theoretical present. Nevertheless, the edition does express the
spirit of Graff's proposal. In an autobiographical passage in *Beyond the*

*Culture Wars,* Graff describes his own formation as a student of literature in these terms. "I like to think I have a certain advantage as a teacher of literature because when I was growing up I disliked and feared books. My youthful aversion to books showed a fine impartiality, extending across the whole spectrum of literature, history, philosophy, and what by then (the late 1940's) had come to be called social studies."[24] He goes on to describe how his "interest was aroused" by the critical controversy over the "ending of *The Adventures of Huckleberry Finn.*"[25] Graff became engaged by the quarrels about the interpretation of the novel. It is an interesting confession. Though one doesn't have to draw the conclusion that Graff draws that exposing students (undergraduates as well as graduates) to the conflict of theories and critical assumptions is the best way into the study of literature, it may have contributed to the development of Graff's polemical talents. But not all students have or enjoy such talents, nor are they necessary to the experience of literature.

Debate and discussion may enhance one's interest in and understanding of a work. But without a love of books (not all books), without, that is, a capacity to be moved by *Anna Karenina,* "Tintern Abbey," *The Brothers Karamazov, Othello, A Portrait of a Lady* (my very partial, but not very arbitrary list), the study of literature becomes a condition of alienation. The love of a work is empathy with creative achievement. Students respond to the enthusiasm of teachers for their subject. A teacher in his or her enthusiasm may convey the arguments that critics have about a work, but they are secondary to the love or dislike that the teacher has for the work. "Teaching the conflicts" is a legacy of current obsession with theory or with a certain kind of theorizing and of its alienating effect on the reading of literature.

What does a work require of its readers? The kind of respect that one shows to another person in listening to his ideas and in attending to the manner in which he expresses himself. Even if one wishes to quarrel with the person, decency requires that the effort be made to understand what is being said and its intention. The culture of reader-centered theoretical criticism in the academy is antithetical to such respect. The individual who created the work has lost whatever authority he had; authority has been transferred to the reader and his or her interests. Since the intelligent reader is never passive (not all readers are intelligent), he will always be in some degree appropriative, but the *intelligent* activity in the reader also requires resistance to one's appropriative impulses. What we read may cause us to reflect on our own views, to hesitate in passing judgment on others, to revise our own ideas. This can occur only if we don't assume automatically that we are morally or ideologically superior to what we read. (We of course may be, when we read a work that defends slavery or the inferiority of women or genocide, but even then we need to calibrate our responses, to sort out what is and what is not of interest and value in works that contain what we believe to be abhorrent views.) I have expressed my reservations about the employment of the term canon in literary studies. I prefer "tradition," because it represents change as well as continuity, whereas canon has the connotation of theological fixity. But we may be stuck with canon, and it has the interesting advantage or disadvantage of evoking the idea of authority. So the question becomes: Do we need the authority implied in the canon of classic works? Authority may be an arbitrary construction, the historical work of an elite, but it may be necessary to the economy of the psyche. For our intellectual formation, we need to read works of superior intelligence and complexity, so that our minds will gain in strength and complexity. We need to learn from these works what is lacking in our emotional as well as intellectual development. We read then not so much for confirmation of what we already know or believe, or of what others would have us believe, but to think against ourselves. Such a view of the canon is at odds with identity politics in which texts are chosen in order to assure the reader that he can find himself or herself in the text. Readers may find themselves in the text, but in ways unpredictable by the prevailing theoretical agendas.

IV

David Denby reports in *Great Books* that Professor Edward Taylor announced to his class that "these books [the classics] will form you"(43). The "you," of course, has an existence prior to whatever formation the books will effect—and that existence already has a form or forms. So Taylor must mean that they will reform or perhaps form what is still inchoate in the students. His challenging remark passes over a source of great contention in literary studies: the nature of the self.

The challenge to this view has many sources. We might begin with modern literature in which the protagonist begins as a stranger to his society or becomes one. The list of books I assigned in my course in "Readings in the Short Novel" is proof enough: *The Death of Ivan Ilych, Notes from Underground, The Metamorphosis, Death in Venice, Heart of Darkness, The Dead, The Man Who Died,* and *The Stranger.* Each of the books is a modern classic, which is to say different from the ancient classics Professor Taylor teaches. And an important difference lies in the character of the protagonist who ends, however he may start out, as a social pariah. Tolstoy's Ivan Ilych and Mann's Aschenbach begin as integral members of their society only to become estranged from it by illness and passion. The underground man is introduced as an outsider and persists to the end in declaring his corrosive vision of the emptiness of society. Kafka's story begins with a transformation of its protagonist, Gregor Samsa, from an uneasy social existence into an alien creature who must be destroyed and exorcised from social memory. And Camus's stranger, affectless and amoral, acquires the passion to affirm his natural self and embraces society's hatred of him. These are characters readers do not come to despise. However repulsive they may be to the ordinary moral sense, they appear to be bearers of some perverse spiritual truth. Unlike the protagonist in the classic works of antiquity or the Renaissance, the modern protagonist is never integrated into society. The reader contemplates the spectacle of the protagonist's ordeal, perhaps with ambivalence; it is unclear how the story forms the reader. The formation, envisaged by the ancient classics, involves a reintegration in the human community. (Oedipus, expelled from Thebes, after the discovery of his parricide and incest, achieves an apotheosis within sight of Athens and becomes its saint.) The path of the modern hero, in contrast, is often death and dissolution.

In its literature and its theory, postmodernism challenges the integrity of both the text and the self. Coherence and unity suggest the repression of multiple energies in the self. The integral self resists the playfulness of role playing, the *jouissance* of erotic expression, as the French would say. To liberate the self is to free it from the constraints of boundaries that coherence and unity imply. A cynic might say that the Eriksonian idea of an identity crisis that had become fashionable decades ago has turned into a "normative" theory of the self.

The most impressive and provocative of postmodern theorists of text and self is Roland Barthes, particularly in *S/Z* (1970), by now a "classic" of postmodernism. (I put classic in quotation marks, because the very idea of a classic is inimical to Barthes and postmodernism.) He takes as his text a minor tale *Sarrasine*, by a classic author, Balzac, in order to wrest authority from the author and bestow it on the reader. To do so, he must break up the text into lexical units, which he then exposes to five major codes under which all the textual signifiers can be grouped: the hermeneutic, the semantic, the symbolic, the proairetic (which refers to plot or action), and the cultural. These are familiar terms of understanding and they are supposed to contribute to an impression of structuralist rigor in reading. But that is not where Barthes's postmodernist appeal lies. Reading for Barthes is the explosion of the text in which the reader experiences pleasure (*jouissance*) rather than acquiring meanings through interpretation. The reader becomes the writer or rewriter of the text in the wake of the death of the author. The Aristotelian teleology of beginning, middle, and end is shattered. The replete and seamless classic work is emptied, the space it leaves to be filled by the reader's own transgressive vitality and pleasure. (*Sarrasine* is a mystery story in which the secret, disclosed at the end, is that the hero's beloved, La Zambinella, is not what "she" appears to be: She is a castrato, a figure of absence, and one assumes, an emblem of Barthes's theory of the text.) The text, on this reading, is a play of signifiers, signifying nothing. "[T]he character is a product of combinations: the combination is relatively stable (denoted by the recurrence of the semes) and more or less complex (involving more or less contradictory figures; the complexity determines the character's 'personality,' which is just as much a combination as the odor of a dish or the bouquet of a wine)."[26] By making us aware of the combination of semes, Barthes means to expose the constructedness of character and its linguistic substance (character is constituted by semes). He means to disabuse us of the view of the self as natural and capable of organic development. But beyond that he wants to deconstruct the "solidarities" that compose the self (not only character, but the self that reads the text).[27] For the "readerly I," that is, the ideal reader required by the classic, "everything holds together." Reading must replicate the integrity of the text. Barthes forestalls the readerly acquiescence to the work by disaggregating the text into lexical units before the reader has a chance to read *Sarrasine*.

The readerly for Barthes becomes anathema, and so he substitutes the word writerly for the act of reading he means to affirm. And what is the writerly but the erotic and liberating dissemination of the self? This, it would appear, is the opposite of forming or shaping the self in the act of reading. In his introduction to *S/Z*, Richard Howard offers a different view. Barthes is asserting a paradox. "Only when we know—and it is knowledge gained by taking pains, by renouncing what Freud calls instinctual gratification—what we are doing when we read, are we free to enjoy what we read."[28] And yet the reading that is anathema to Barthes is reading in a "repressed and repressive way . . . which fences us in, closes us off."[29] On this view, the renunciation of instinct gratification is opposed to repression! Howard's logic may be dubious, but he has caught hold of the sophisticated and deliberate character of Barthes's imaginative anarchism. The act of disintegrating or multiplying the self is hard work. It is transgressive, perhaps even coercive, not the instinctive expression of our natural selves.

It would be a mistake, however, to dismiss this conception of the "self" (which requires enclosure in quotation marks) to postmodern perversity. It is an enacted theme in modern literature—in the character of Leopold Bloom, for instance, whose imagination in the nighttown episode of *Ulysses* produces multiple and contradictory versions of himself: voyeur, masochist, reformer, mayor of Dublin, emperor of Ireland. Who is to say that Bloom's fantasies of himself are simply illusions and not expressions of his "real self"? Which is not to say that the disintegration of the self is necessarily an occasion for celebration. More often than not it is a reason for despair. Dowell, the feckless hero of Ford Madox Ford's *The Good Soldier*, speculates despairingly about the disappearance of character from modern society.

For who in this world can give anyone a character? Who in this world knows anything of any other heart—or his own? I don't mean to say that one cannot form an average estimate of the way a person will behave. But one cannot be certain of the way any man will behave in every case—and until one can do that a "character" is of no use to anyone.[30]

By character Dowell and (I assume) Ford mean the moral intelligibility of the self. Speaking of Leonora's discovery of her husband's infidelities, Dowell makes a revealing qualification: "if you like to call them infidelities," in effect signaling to his readers that the inherited moral vocabulary on which character depends and which depends on it will no longer serve. He is describing the disappearance of the morally coherent self at an historical moment.

And what is the attitude toward the fragmented self at our historical moment? In Philip Roth's *The Counterlife*, the writer hero, Nathan Zuckerman, Roth's stand-in, so to speak, proposes the theory that some people are "divided in themselves," a condition that "the whole Western idea of mental health" tries to redeem by establishing an ideal of the "congruity between your self-consciousness and your natural being." Zuckerman challenges the realist assumption of "a natural being, an irreducible self. . . . If there even *is* a natural being, an irreducible self, it is rather small, I think, and may even be the root of all impersonation—the natural being may be the skill itself, the innate capacity to impersonate." It follows "that I, for one, have no self. . . . What I have instead is a variety of impersonations I can do, and not only of myself— a troupe of players that I have internalized, a permanent company of actors that I can call upon when a self is required, an ever-evolving stock of pieces and parts that form my repertoire."[31] This is a ludic Zuckerman, imagining himself as a multiplicity of roles in which the quiddity of an authentic self evaporates.

In Roth's recent novel, *American Pastoral*, however, a darker view emerges. The hero, Swede Levov, observes with astonishment "how people seemed to run out of their own being, run out of whatever the stuff was that made them who they were and, drained of themselves, turn into the sort of people they would have felt sorry for. It was as though while their lives were rich and full they were secretly sick of themselves and couldn't wait to dispose of their sanity and their health and all sense of proportion so as to get down to that other self, the *true* self, who was a wholly deluded fuckup."[32] Levov has a vision of the emptying out of the substantial self. Unlike *The Counterlife*, *American Pastoral* does not promise liberation.

There is a paradox in the postmodern conception of identity. On the one hand, postmodernism affirms the coherent identities of racial and ethnic groups, and, on the other hand, it deconstructs the idea of a coherent personal identity. Identity obtains in cultural politics, but not in personal psychology. But even this formulation needs to be qualified, for what we are experiencing now is an unprecedented obsession with autobiography and personal memoir—as if writers are trying to recuperate from the fragmentation of their beings and experience some sense of coherence. I have characterized the effect of the classic as disturbance and possibly reformation of the self. But if, as the postmoderns tell us, we lack the integrity of a self, or to put it more conditionally, *when* we lack the integrity, a premodern classic may be a way of focusing the self, of providing a sense of identity, if only provisionally.

If the classics are to form readers, they will have to contend not only with the formidable array of forces in contemporary life (its violence and distractions), but with the persuasive powers of modern literature as well.

# 4

၆/၆

# "All That Is Solid Melts into the Air"
## Popular Culture and the Academy

Don DeLillo's novel *White Noise* is set in a college town. It is one of the sites where our postmodern sense of reality is manufactured, the others being the supermarket and the media world of cinema and television. And indeed, television itself becomes for Murray Siskind, the charismatic instructor at the college, the principal medium of instruction. His colleague, Jack Gladney, who narrates the novel, tries to protect his son against television, so that he will grow up "intelligent and literate." But even he worries that he may then be "depriving his son of the deeper codes and messages that mark his species as unique."[1] In effect, he concedes the argument to Siskind, who affirms the codes and messages of our media-dominated culture:

TV is a problem only if you've forgotten how to look and listen. . . . My students and I discuss this all the time. They're beginning to feel they ought to turn against the medium, exactly as an earlier generation turned against their parents and their country. I tell them they have to learn to look as children again. Root out content. Find the codes and messages, to use your phrase, Jack.[2]

And what is that content? "TV offers incredible amounts of psychic data. It opens ancient memories of world birth, it welcomes us into the grid, the network of little buzzing dots that make up the picture pattern." Siskind characterizes the experience as "almost mystical."

When asked what view he takes of the characters and events in his novels, DeLillo says he is neutral. He means neither to parody nor to celebrate. But in the characterization of Siskind he does manage to con-

86

vey the excitement of an intelligent man about his new subject. DeLillo is representing a phenomenon of the contemporary academy, the embrace of popular culture as a source of knowledge of the world.

What is interesting about Siskind's response to television is its mandarin character, a high cultural sensibility seduced by the products of popular culture. One thinks of camp, with its emphasis on style, the "aesthetic" experience of popular culture. A difference may be the absence of irony in the academy. Camp condescended in its embrace of its object; its attitude guaranteed that it would not become an excuse for kitsch. Style was of the essence in camp. Siskind is not without style, but he strikes a note of seriousness or solemnity that reflects the approach of actual practitioners in the academy.

The antihumanism of the Siskind view is clear in his debate with Gladney about how human beings should face death. The exchange between Gladney and Siskind is more catechism than debate, in which Siskind's questions provoke answers that disabuse Gladney of his humanist illusions.

"Doesn't our knowledge of death make life more precious?"

"What good is a preciousness based on fear and anxiety? It's an anxious quivering thing. . . ."

"A person has to be told he is going to die before he can live life to the fullest. True or false?"

"False. Once your death is established, it becomes impossible to live a satisfying life."[3]

The whole humanist tradition has as one of its beliefs that life achieves an intensity of experience in the awareness of our mortality. It is the wisdom of Greek tragedy. Montaigne says to philosophize is to learn how to die. And the dying of Tolstoy's Ivan Ilych becomes a kind of rebirth. To avert your eyes from your mortal condition is paradoxically a death-in-life.

But postmodern Siskind will have none of it:

You could put your faith in technology. It got you here, it can get you out. This is the whole point of technology. It creates an appetite for immortality. . . . It's what we invented to conceal the terrible secret of our decaying bodies. But it's also life, isn't it? It prolongs life, it provides new organs for those that wear out. . . .[4]

Technology also enables us to contemplate death as a spectacle that never touches us. Here is Siskind on the car crash in the movies:

> I tell [my students] that they can't think of a car crash in a movie as a violent act. It's a celebration. A reaffirmation of traditional values and beliefs. I connect car crashes to holidays like Thanksgiving and the Fourth. We don't mourn the dead or rejoice in miracles. These are days of secular optimism, of self-celebration. . . . Watch any car crash in any American movie. It is a high-spirited moment. . . . The people who stage these crashes are able to capture a lightheartedness. . . .[5]

This is a celebration of the aestheticizing or, perhaps more accurately, the anesthetizing of violence and suffering, the daily experience of television watching.

Popular culture has become not simply another subject for study; it now challenges the authority—or what used to be the authority—of the academic culture of books. If what the student needs is information to get on in our "global" economy, he would do better to go to the internet than to the library or bookstore; a stroke of the key on the computer can yield him the kind of data that he needs in a relatively short time. In his "Defense of Poetry," Shelley lamented the wisdom lost in information. He foresaw our computer age. Siskind would say that there is a wisdom to be learned if we knew how to decode the messages of popular culture, root out its content. The world is changing in radical and exciting ways, this new wisdom declares, and the academy better get with it. In fact, it already has.

There is a political dimension to the presence of popular culture in the academy that connects with its current devotion to ideology critique. Like ideology, popular culture is an elusive term with a protean history. For Richard Hoggart, the distinguished cultural historian and inspirer of the Birmingham Center for Cultural Studies, popular culture needed to be distinguished from mass culture ("popular" having its roots in provincial or working-class life, "mass" in the commercialization and standardization of culture). "Popular" referred to a country ballad, "mass" to advertising, and so on. For Hoggart, "popular" was friend, "mass" foe. There was no antipathy between popular and high culture. On the contrary, what Hoggart calls "working-class culture" (before the assault of

modern technology) was congenial to high cultural values. Hoggart himself was a scion of the working class and his desire to read English at
Leeds University and become a university professor was a fulfillment, not
a betrayal. Hoggart's contemporary, the critic F. R. Leavis, used to emphasize the cultural richness of provincial life, which nurtured the imaginations of George Eliot, Thomas Hardy, and D. H. Lawrence. A sort of
reciprocity existed between high culture and popular culture. Think of
T. S. Eliot's visits to the musical hall (which he commemorated in his
essay on the music hall singer Marie Lloyd) and whose notes sound
through his poetry. The traffic of popular culture to high culture did not
erase the distinction between the two cultures; they remained high and
popular.

Popular culture used to be a regional culture. As the globalization
of the economy proceeds and with it the global commercialization of culture, the very existence of regional popular culture becomes more and
more a vestige of the past. T. S. Eliot, who wrote before the concept and
practice of globalization came into existence, understood nevertheless
that the cosmopolitan spirit of modernism should not unfold at the expense of regional cultures. In *Notes Toward a Definition of Culture*,
Eliot speaks of the need for diversity as well as unity. The unity of cosmopolitanism is not the resultant of the forces of diversity, but rather a
dimension (world literature, for example) that transcends it.

The distinction between "popular" and "mass" has disappeared in
contemporary discourse, if not in reality. "Popular" is the preferred
word, in our democratic ethos, since it does not have the invidious asso-
ciations evoked by "mass." Perhaps it is an inevitable development of democratization that the "popular" no longer knows its place. It has become
an antagonist of high culture and the intellectuals who defend it. Or at
least this is one kind of discourse that has emerged in the academy.

The work of Andrew Ross, the editor of the postmodern journal *Social Text*, is a revealing example of the politicizing of popular culture.
Ross's book *No Respect: Intellectuals and Popular Culture* (the title is
taken from the whining refrain of the comedian Rodney Dangerfield, "I
get no respect") begins with a story comedian Bill Cosby tells about his
ambivalent relationship to authority and Rodney Dangerfield's pose as
an intellectual in the movie *Back to School* (1986), which Ross reads as

a parable about "intellectual and popular culture, authority and disrespect, hegemony and consent."[6]

Ross's study of popular culture quickly becomes a demystification of the intellectuals who define "what is popular and legitimate taste, who supervise the passports, the temporary visas, the cultural identities, the threatening 'alien' elements, and the deportation orders, and who occasionally make their own adventurist forays across the border."[7] Not exactly perspicuous prose (what "adventurist forays"?), but it is clear from the passage and elsewhere with its talk about "cultural power" and "polic[ing] in the differentiated middle ground" that Foucault's categories of surveillance and discipline haunt Ross's book. Popular culture becomes in Ross's account the site of resistance not only to the disciplinary power of intellectuals, but also to intellectuals, who by their very nature are conservative. A study of popular culture turns into a scrutiny of the politics of the Cold War. The first two chapters are entitled "Reading the Rosenberg Letters" and "Containing Culture in the Cold War."

Ross begins by attacking the responses of "cold war intellectuals" to the Rosenberg phenomenon, in particular Leslie Fiedler's "close reading" of the letters between Ethel and Julius, in which the inauthenticity of the feelings in the letters become evidence of their guilt. Ross has a point. (I myself reviewed Fiedler's *An End to Innocence* when it came out and found bizarre the recourse to literary criticism in the life-and-death matter of the Rosenbergs' guilt or innocence.) And Ross may also be right that the effect of turning the Rosenbergs into an emblem of Communist corruption had the effect of dehumanizing them. But in declaring that there was only flimsy evidence against the Rosenbergs without displaying any expertise about the trial, he is little more than an ideologue. And what does this have to do with popular culture?

But the Rosenbergs did not *exist* [for Fiedler], inasmuch as their existence only had meaning for the Stalinized mind, for which events and persons do not *exist* until they appear in Party journals and newspapers. Fiedler imagines a small group of "conscious exploiters" in the Party, manipulating a "mass of naive communicants" who form a conveniently "prefabricated public," thereby "stalinized at second or third remove." But this stereotyped picture of American Communists as slavish automatons of foreign directives hardly does justice to the flourishing of a political community and subculture which, in the thirties and forties, had transformed so many thousands of its members' lives and which, in the Popular Front period, had tried to establish deep roots in American political institutions, cultural traditions, and popular structures of feeling. In fact, the inadequacy of this scenario makes it virtually indistinguishable from the conspiracy picture of American industrial mass culture, made familiar by Clement Greenberg, Dwight MacDonald, and other Cold War liberals— whereby the fat cat capitalist "lords of kitsch" set about ventriloquizing an inert and prefabricated mass of consumers.[8]

As someone who grew up in the "Stalinized" community to which Ross refers, I feel confident in saying that he exhibits no real knowledge of this community. Anybody who has seriously read the literature of the period (one needn't have experienced it directly) knows how manipulative the party was in directing the thought and actions not only of its members, but also of the more benign organizations that fronted for the party. And precisely what does Ross mean by "a political community and subculture" trying "to establish deep roots in American political institutions and popular structures of feeling"? He provides not a single example. The subculture with which I was familiar were the novels of Howard Fast, songs of the Spanish Civil War and the Red Army, hootenannies, and not very distinguished Yiddish stories and poems of Jewish suffering. There *were* very talented performers such as Paul Robeson and Pete Seeger. Ross's characterization of the community and the period is remote from any lived reality. The concluding jibe at Clement Greenberg and Dwight MacDonald, ideologically reduced to Cold War liberals, seems singularly inept. (What is the relevance of characterizing the attack on capitalist kitsch as that of Cold War liberals?) Perhaps Ross is trying to show that he is evenhanded in condemning all conspiracy theories, whether the target is Communist or capitalist.

Ross's own conspiracy picture is of elitist academic intellectuals and Cold War liberals trying to contain popular culture. His strategy is to put the "tastemaking intellectuals" on the defensive in every situation in which high culture and popular culture are at odds. Here is what he has to say about Susan Sontag's essay "Notes on Camp" (1964):

Susan Sontag raises the question of survival in a quite specific way: "Camp is the answer to the problem: how to be a dandy in an age of mass culture." Her formula suggests that what is being threatened in an age of mass culture is precisely the power of tastemaking intellectuals to influence the canons of taste, and that the significance of the "new sensibility" of camp in the sixties is that it is a means of salvaging that privilege. (The term "dandy," here, can be seen as standing for intellectuals who are either personally devoted to the sophistries of taste, or whose intellectual work it is to create, legitimize and supervise canons of taste.)[9]

Ross's prose is marked with resentment toward what he regards as the elitist pretensions of the tastemaking intellectuals ("a means of salvaging . . . privilege," devotion "to the sophistries of taste"). Does Ross resent the particular tastes of these intellectuals (no attempt is made to characterize them and test their claims), or does he resent the very process of tastemaking?

Apparently, the latter:

Pop arose out of problematizing the question of *taste* itself, and, in its purist forms, was addressed directly to the media processes through which cultural taste is defined and communicated. Not only did it deny the imposition from above, of seeming arbitrary boundaries of taste, but it also questioned the distanced contemplation, interpretive expertise, and categories of aesthetic judgment which accompanies that imposition. Nothing could be more execrable to a tradition of taste that was founded on the precepts of "universality," "timelessness," and "uniqueness" than a culture of obsolescence: i.e. specifically designed not to endure.[10]

There is an unremarked paradox in the fact that the culture of obsolescence is a universal or global culture. Disney, McDonald's, Coca-Cola, action films, the internet are everywhere. What we have now is a combination of universality and ephemerality. The rapid obsolescence of computers is a vivid example of our global culture. I doubt whether practitioners of pop art would choose to recognize themselves in the academic jargon word "problematizing." It would seem to be contrary to the very spirit of pop. Rather than problematizing or questioning, would it not be more accurate to say it challenges or defies taste? And so where does it leave us? Apparently with a tasteless culture, only too willing to consume itself in planned obsolescence. Pop art on its own account has no more value than the badly made Fords and Chevrolets that filled the market in the 1980s and the 1990s. Its authenticity derives not from anything intrinsic to it, but from its demystifying wisdom that all impositions from above are arbitrary and that "universality," "timelessness," and "uniqueness" are no more than words enclosed in quotation marks.

The idea of "a throwaway culture"[11] (a culture of obsolescence) does an injustice to the enduring pleasures of popular culture. The pleasure we take in watching a baseball or football or basketball game, an episode of *Seinfeld*, a Woody Allen movie endures in the sense that we return to them again and again. Our appreciation depends on a knowledge of the tradition of the games and of the fables which the TV and the movie narrative unfold. And they are pleasures that don't require the subversion of the achievement of high culture.

What is remarkable about Ross's description of the ideology of pop is that it is also an endorsement. So powerful is the animus against the tastemaking intellectuals that he, like his pop icons, is willing to embrace "a throwaway culture." Any ambition to produce a work of art that might endure is seen, from this politicized perspective, as an effort to contain and discipline energies that ought to be liberated, liberation understood here as entropy. This is a far cry from traditional popular culture, which produced, for example, folk ballads of enduring fame. The analogy that I made between pop art and the American automobile industry is not fortuitous, for it is part of the project of pop art and its academic acolytes to *identify* the making of art with the marketplace. Andy Warhol is exemplary for this way of thinking about art. Warhol describes his art as a "recycling of leftover things." "You're recycling work and you're recycling people, you're running your business as a byproduct of other businesses. Of other *directly competitive* businesses, as a matter of fact."[12] Ross comments that Warhol's "attention to *economy* was more than just a metaphor for the critique of capitalism that all art must surely deliver from its autonomous heart. It suggests that art had something more directly to do with products, consumers and markets than it had to do with fighting the 'good fight' or with the aesthete's mindless realm of great art."[13] Pop art in other words takes us beyond the consideration (hard to gainsay) that the marketplace is a setting for the activity of art to the aesthetically nihilist proposition that it is the very essence of art. Furthermore, pop art does not simply declare its own market essence; it means to generalize the view to all art. Ross relishes the accomplishment: "As for what Warhol refers to as the inherent 'funniness' of leftovers, that is the other side of camp—the creamy wit, the wicked fantasies, and the gaieté de coeur. All that was, and still is, priceless."

There is of course an irony in the fact that Warhol and other pop artists have entered the museum, the site of enduring art, and command the high prices that presuppose the persistence of their value. (The high prices tell us that consumer capitalism has a place for permanence.) Warhol spoke of fifteen minutes of fame as the postmodern condition of celebrity. But his fame has lasted more than fifteen minutes, as have his Campbell soup cans and his Marilyn Monroes. It cannot be said in his defense that this is not what he intended, for Warhol has shown himself to be complicit with the cultural forces that work to make his art endure. The issue here is not whether the art deserves to endure, but the inextinguishable desire for permanence.

Ross writes as if the bastions of high culture are still formidable, whereas by his own account the tastemaking intellectuals are in retreat and may even have lost much of their confidence. The larger culture of which the academy has become a part is the scene of triumph of popular culture:

Today, as the cult of knowledge and expertise presides over the internationalization of the information revolution, and the universities absorb all forms of intellectual activity, it is equally clear that the mantle of opposition no longer rests upon the shoulders of an autonomous avant-garde, neither the elite metropolitan intellectuals who formed the traditional corpus of public tastemakers or opinionmakers; nor the romantic neo-bohemians who shaped the heroic image of the unattached dissenter. . . .[14]

It is not enough that the enemy has already been defeated; Ross wants to help bury him. There is evidently no value in preserving within the academy an enclave for the bohemian, the dissenting intellectual, the tastemaker—or, for that matter, rational intelligence. If there is opposition, it will come from "popular histories and popular culture," increasingly attentive "to the experience of women, people of color, gays and lesbians," all victims of oppression, and the objects of opposition will be "the traditional idealist histories, histories which depict moral struggles waged by heroic individuals in order to save Western civilization from successive 'barbarisms.'"[15]

Popular culture has become the scene of race, gender, ethnicity, and sexual preference. It is for Ross and other pop cultists above all the scene for unconstrained bodily and sexual experiences, and the genre of choice is pornography. Against the "appointed or self-styled intellectual protectors of the public interest," Ross proposes the following utopian prospect:

> In contrast to the case of realist entertainment, where a film can draw criticism because it is "too unrealistic" or far-fetched, pornography can be criticized for a surfeit of realism which brings its fantasy uncomfortably close to home. So, too, it is likely that the porn film spectacle of hard-working bodies, repetitiously pursuing, with muscle and sweat and sperm, the performance and productivity levels required by the genre has as much to do with the libidinal economy of labor as with the popular aesthetic of athletic prowess. In this respect, the use of pornography might be said to challenge any tidy division between labor and leisure, or productivity and pleasure; its use speaks, at some level, to the potential power of fantasy to locate pleasure in work (even to eroticize work) as well as in play.[16]

Ross provides us with an unwitting parody of Herbert Marcuse's dream of an eroticized civilization. Who would have thought that pornography would be its vehicle?

It also needs to be said that Ross and others have not simply brought popular culture into the academy for their political purposes. In a sense they have brought the academy into popular culture. How else to account for the fact that the academy has imitated Hollywood in becoming the site of celebrity? We now speak of academics as stars and superstars. The medium of performance is theory, and the more outlandishly formulated the theory, the greater the chance of success in gaining the attention of the media, where stars are made. Even when the press is hostile, as it has been toward the Duke University English Department, the attention it has received has had the effect of putting it on the map. New theories of cultural politics (in feminism, African American, and gay and lesbian studies) have registered and effected changes in attitudes and discourse in our cultural life. It would be expected for the media to report them. What I am suggesting is that the reporting, rarely serious, often falls under the category of entertainment in which popular performers of the academy are complicit. For them a bad review is better than indifference.

II

Ross's approach is not anomalous in the profession, though his pop bias gives it an unusual edge. In following Fredric Jameson's injunction—"Always historicize!"—students of the aesthetic have in effect reduced it to the motives of the marketplace. What begins as an effort to show the historical conditions in which certain ideas emerge becomes an argument that all ideas are ultimately tethered to those conditions and that our understanding of them is impoverished when we separate them in order to consider their intrinsic character. The historicizing of aesthetic ideas turns into a justification for a relativistic aesthetics in which all judgments have equal value, or, in the words of the nineteenth-century utilitarian Francis Jeffrey:

It is a strange aberration indeed of vanity that makes us despise persons for being happy—for having sources of enjoyment in which we cannot share;—and yet this is the true account of the ridicule we bestow upon individuals who seek only to enjoy their peculiar tastes unmolested;—for, if there be any truth in the theory we have been expounding, no taste is bad for any other reason than because it is peculiar—as the objects in which it delights must actually serve to suggest to the individual those common emotions and universal affections upon which the sense of beauty is everywhere founded.[17]

Beauty exists, but it differs from perceiver to perceiver, and the effort to impose one's own taste on others reflects arrogance and intolerance, a foreshadowing of reader-centered criticism.

In *Author, Art, and the Market: Rereading the History of Aesthetics,* Martha Woodmansee speaks of Jeffrey's "resounding affirmation of diversity" as a reflection of his "confidence" in the free market of culture. It is "a theory of art that affirms art's complete integration into an economy in which the value of an object is a function of its utility to consumers who cannot be wrong—except by consuming too little."[18] By itself the sentence does not disclose Woodmansee's view of Jeffrey's theory. We suspect that diversity is a value for her, but that the idea of art as fully integrated into capitalist economy might be suspect, given her (Marxist?) materialist approach to aesthetics. Isn't she demystifying an aesthetics that identifies itself with the marketplace? Apparently not, for

her main animus is reserved for Coleridge, who in attacking philosophical associationism (the basis for Jeffrey's utilitarian aesthetic) shows
himself, in Woodmansee's account, as an arrogant obscurantist, whose
Kantian belief in the autonomy of art (i.e., its independence of the diversity of perception and judgment it might provoke) "cannot have con-
vinced many readers" with his "barrage of specialized terms."[19]

In the demystifying fashion characteristic of our moment, Woodmansee reads Coleridge's Kantianism as a sort of compensation for the
public's indifference to his and Wordsworth's writing. Never once does
she consider the intrinsic and radical deficiencies of a theory that declares that "no taste is bad" (recall Bentham's notorious dictum: "Poetry
is equal to pushpin"). Whatever Coleridge's motive (or that of any other
Kantian theorist) might have been, there is an argument to be made for
aesthetic and intellectual standards that deserves to be taken seriously
and not approached in a debunking spirit. It is something of an irony
that the cultural left (and Woodmansee's book as well as Ross's is an example) has imbibed the demystifying spirit of capitalism in its approach
to matters intellectual and aesthetic. Alan Wolfe has remarked how the
exponents of popular culture on the left have in effect embraced the
spirit of capitalism, but has anyone remarked that Marx himself learned
to be demystifying from his study of the way capitalism in its emergence
from a feudal economy reduced everything to the cash nexus?

How do these approaches, the aesthetic and the market, differ in
practice when they engage serious fiction? I can illustrate the differences
in the work of two recent critics of Henry James, who fortuitously share
the name of Bell: Millicent and Ian. These Bells make different sounds.
Millicent Bell gives us the music of James, its internal logic, which in
criticism we first hear in Percy Lubbock's *The Craft of Fiction.* Ian Bell
provides a more up-to-date, market-oriented James in the service of an
economy of consumption. Which is not to say that Millicent Bell
doesn't provide us with fresh analytic perspectives, especially on the
matter of plot, or that Ian Bell is utterly impervious to the literary character of James's achievement (he in fact refers generously to Millicent
Bell's work), but the sensibilities at play in these two works are contrasting sensibilities. They offer us an opportunity to reflect on alternative approaches to literary study.

The argument of Millicent Bell's study concentrates on the disparity that James perceived between the potentialities of self and the limiting conditions of social existence. In narrative terms, this translates into a dissonance between character and plot. James's protagonists (Isabel Archer, Hyacinth Robinson, Lambert Strether), surrogates for his own imagination of possibility, experience plot, which for Aristotle is the very soul of drama, as inimical to their fulfillment, because plot threatens to degrade the self to material and social forms or to confine it to a single outcome and therefore rob it of its multifariousness. Bell notes how in reviewing his notebooks James rediscovered possibilities and outcomes for his stories that he had passed by, and how he regretted the suppressed alternatives that characterize any individual life. But, as Bell convincingly demonstrates, without the enactment of character in a story, the potentiality of character turns into impotence and poverty. John Marcher of *The Beast in the Jungle* becomes, from this perspective, the *reductio ad absurdum* of the self's effort to maintain the fullness of its potentiality. True to the spirit of James, Bell does not attempt to resolve this ambiguity: "[T]he gesture, the dream, the withholding of commitment to social forms that reduced the soul's best potential, this *is* a vision that takes account—by rejection— of a reducing reality, though the vision of freedom which imbues an Isabel Archer is proven to be an illusion."[20] The ambiguity is sustained by a continual and tantalizing deferral of a commitment to a particular outcome, and by inviting the reader, so Bell argues, to resist totalizing interpretations and to make a "succession of interpretations based on instant states."[21] This corresponds to the drama of Strether's consciousness in *The Ambassadors*, but it should apply elsewhere in James's work.

The Jamesian narrative, according to Millicent Bell, thrives in the tension between an Emersonian aspiration for transcendence and a European-inspired knowledge of the limiting conditions of existence. The pathos of James's fiction derives from the exacerbation rather than the resolution of the tension. Milly Theale of *The Wings of the Dove* embodies this tension:

It is Milly who must finally face the inevitability of her own death, must realize— sooner and more sharply than most persons—that the mere fact of being human exposes one to circumscriptions more absolute than poverty. Still, her ability to act freely persists. She asserts the survival of her own potentiality, asserts

James's romantic faith in the human will, acting even in her dying to fulfill her own curious prediction, "since I've lived all *these* years as if I were dead, I shall die no doubt, as if I were alive."[22]

The received wisdom about James is that he inverted the Aristotelian hierarchy which privileges plot over character. But Millicent Bell shows with great subtlety how plot, in its various meanings of intrigue, conspiracy, and narrative, works in contradictory fashion to test, oppose, and reveal character. One casualty of the Jamesian narrative is the marriage plot, which no longer promises the happy resolution that one finds in much of Victorian "realist" fiction. Marriage does not close *Portrait of a Lady;* it fails in the middle of the novel and makes possible Isabel Archer's awareness of the inhospitality of the world to the dream of plenitude. The effect of Bell's reading is to make character and plot, the main constituents of narrative, the very content of James's fiction. Without losing connection to realism, the novels become allegories of the making of fiction.

Despite his several admiring references to the work of Millicent Bell, Ian Bell's focus is elsewhere. His study oscillates between the Jamesian text and the consumer marketplace that emerged at the time of James's writing (1832–1860). The logic of James's imagination, according to Ian Bell, participates in the logic of the marketplace. Thus *Washington Square* is an arena for competing market forces. Catherine Sloper, "the commodified Catherine, worth 'eighty thousand a year,'" becomes the object of a competition among her father Dr. Sloper, her housekeeper Mrs. Penniman, and her suitor Townsend, "within the frozen world of market practice." Bell wants us "to see an intimate relationship between forms of writing, forms of history and forms of financial behavior."[23] He does not declare his motive to be demystification of the moral–aesthetic idiom of the Jamesian text, but something like it seems to be at work when he chides other critics for discussing Townsend as a "heartless lover" or "an interloper," since "such categorization inevitably seals him off from material history."[24]

The effect of such an approach is to displace our focus from the moral ambition of the fiction to its alleged complicity with what one may presume to be the very target of its criticism. At least this is the presumption of Millicent Bell when she writes about *Wings of the Dove:*

In this novel James presents through symbolic action and language the reflex of a commercial society in the recesses of public life. With extraordinary insight into the nature of modern experience, he recognizes that it is not sufficiently descriptive of modern man to say that he is subject to a market economy and constantly engaged in a contest for economic advantage. The competitive establishment of market value extends to those parts of a person, those aspects of behavior, once thought to have *incalculable* value.[25]

Ian Bell is concerned with exposing what he believes to be the inadequacy of oppositions such as the calculable and the incalculable, the public and the private, given the imperializing force of the marketplace. Thus in his description of *The Bostonians* he speaks of "publicity [as] the agency whereby the world advertises and perpetuates itself," a "synecdoche for the changing culture in which all his characters are caught up." All that James can manage in the way of critique is an expression of distaste, "which fails to incorporate the diagnostic complexity we find in the fiction."[26]

Ian Bell's account of the self in relation to society turns out to be quite different from Millicent Bell's. The self has lost its capacity for resistance; indeed, it seems to have lost its quiddity, becoming instead a function of the dynamism, the fluidity, the transformations of the marketplace. The private and the personal in a sense cease to exist, since the self has been taken over by publicity. An example is the spectacle of Verena as public performer in *The Bostonians*. Character becomes role; behavior becomes performance. Ian Bell resolves the moral tension that Millicent Bell finds in James's fiction in the determinisms of the marketplace. Ian Bell, following Jean Baudrillard, speaks of a shift that occurs within the culture of consumption, to which James has been assigned the role of inadvertent witness, from the civic to the advertisable, from the public to publicity, the effect of which is to dissolve the person into personality.

Ian Bell's approach flattens the world of Jamesian fiction to one of "display, surface and performance."[27] He speaks of James's ambivalent relation to it, but it would seem to be an ambivalence without force, since he finds so little in the narrative consciousness of the fiction to resist the culture of consumption. Missing from Ian Bell's discussion is the rich interiority, the sense of potentiality that figures so impressively in

Millicent Bell's exposition of the fiction. This is not to deny that he has caught hold of something in his interpretations of *Washington Square*, *The Bostonians*, and *The Europeans*, but the claim he makes hardly does justice to *Portrait of a Lady* or the late novels, which he mercifully does not study at any length.

It used to be an argument in favor of a critical performance that it was responsive to the texture of the work, that it gave back in its own language the idiom and spirit of the work being interpreted. A critic who performs in this manner nowadays is exercising an unfashionable virtue. Millicent Bell's work is clearly the fruit of a long devotion; it is a superbly meditated study, a critical act with the greatest respect for the novelist's achievement. And it is enriched by a resourceful and sophisticated understanding of narrative theory. Ian Bell also admires James, but the terms of his admiration are defined by historical categories (the culture of production and the culture of consumption) that only partially fit the subject and that translate the Jamesian story into someone else's narrative. James's characters become allegorical figures in the triumphant emergence of a consumer culture in America. Even that story is taken for granted as representing a history in which James can be neatly placed and explained. Ian Bell cites a variety of scholarly sources on the culture of consumption, but gives us no clear persuasive account of its character or of what might be contending understandings of it. Ian Bell's study does not satisfy our curiosity about the story or stories that James *tells;* to satisfy our curiosity we turn to Millicent Bell.

Both Ross and Woodmansee, despite differences in their subjects and in their manners, have as their adversary (explicit in the case of Ross, implicit in the cases of Woodmansee and Ian Bell), the taste-making intellectuals, those who believe in the possibility of disinterested reflection and judgment. The effect of translating aesthetic experience into marketplace theory is to resolve a more than century-long tension between high and popular culture into a victory for popular, now mass culture. "All that is solid melts into the air," Marx famously said. The postmodern theorists of popular culture have embraced the saying as gospel and invite us to enjoy the spectacle of our throwaway culture, which now aggrandizes even the achievements of serious art.

In an essay entitled "Humanities in the Age of Money," James Engell and Anthony Dangerfield report the results of two years of research. If "money [is] *the* most desirable result of education," then the humanities must inevitably lose out in competition with the social sciences and the sciences, for they fail to satisfy the following criteria for success:

*A Promise of Money.* The field is popularly linked (even if erroneously) to improved chances of securing an occupation, a profession that promises above average lifetime earning.

*A Knowledge of Money.* The field itself studies money, whether practically or more theoretically, i.e. fiscal, business, financial, or economic matters and markets.

*A Source of Money.* The field receives significant external money, i.e. research contracts, federal grants or funding support or corporate underwriting.[28]

What this interesting article fails to mention is the extent to which the humanities has taken "the knowledge of money" as one of its subjects at the same time that a sort of underclass of temporary or part-time instructors is emerging as a major presence in the academy. "Superstar" professors at very high salaries and low-paid part-time instructors are a recipe for a resentful preoccupation with money. In their failure to address the increasing polarization in the profession, college and university administrators bear a heavy responsibility for the current malaise. The article appears under the heading: "The Market-Model University." What I have been describing is an approach to the humanities that in effect follows the market model. Its deleterious effect is a certain cynicism toward the claim of what had always been an essential part of the humanities—the aesthetic.

# 5

❧

# Does Literary Studies Have a Future?

Does literary studies have a future? This is a question normally asked by those who are unhappy with the present regime in literature departments. But it is a legitimate question for anyone to ask in light of the changes that have occurred in the field in recent decades. The study of the literary work has turned into the study of "the cultural text." The new approach to literature often goes by the name of cultural studies, which in practice means the ideological interpretation of a text. Literary works are not the exclusive purview of cultural studies. Films, television, institutions, whatever qualifies as a cultural event or fact comes under their scrutiny. My focus is on literary study, much of which has become one or another version of ideological interpretation.

Here are some of the questions that exemplify literary discussion in the academy. What is the colonialist argument in *The Tempest*? Is Jane Austen complicit with patriarchy in her celebration of the marriages of her main characters? Is *Heart of Darkness* an imperialist and racist work? Is T. S. Eliot's muse anti-Semitism? For those on the cultural left, politics is, as it were, the repressed truth of literature, which ideology critique liberates. For others, it may be a cause for jeremiads, if not about the death of literature, certainly about the demise of literary study.

The most serious threat to literature comes from popular or mass culture, supported by the ever-increasing power of technology. If college-age students prefer to watch television to reading, and if, as the propagandists for new technology tell us, the computer with its exponentially increasing power to deliver information is where the educational action is, there may be little hope for the serious study of serious literature in

103

the future. One might expect the ideology critics to resist the commercial energies that support popular culture, but in their suspicion of high culture, they have been complicit in weakening its authority. In his recent book, *The Rise and Fall of English*, Robert Scholes, in the spirit of Murray Siskind of DeLillo's *White Noise*, proposes that the discipline of literary studies be transformed into a discipline of textual studies. Literature would be removed from its place of privilege and join other cultural texts such as commercials, television drama, and political speeches as subject matter for the decoding of messages.[1]

It is hyperbole (perhaps necessary hyperbole) to speak of "the death of literature" or even of "the demise of literary studies." There will always be teachers and students with literary sensibility who will persist in reading and responding to literature. And even among those engaged in cultural studies, pleasure in the literary work is not and will not be entirely absent. But there is little doubt that a sea change has occurred in the field at the expense of what has been understood as *literary* study. Hence the mood of despair in the recent work of Harold Bloom and Frank Kermode. In *The Western Canon: The Books and School of the Ages*, Bloom begins and ends with elegiac chapters ("An Elegy for the Canon" and "Elegiac Conclusion"). Bloom's jeremiad is fraught with paradox: a lament over the passing of what was meant for the ages.[2] Kermode, following Bernard Bergonzi, suggests a division of labor, a "split[ing] off [of] conventional literary study from the activity now known as 'cultural studies.'"[3] Kermode echoes Matthew Arnold when he speaks of the literary remainder from the split as a "remnant": "Our remnant will not have an easy time." (In *Culture and Anarchy* and elsewhere, Arnold spoke of individuals, alienated from their class prejudices, who might constitute a remnant of saviors of culture from the prevailing philistinism. He derived the metaphor from the Biblical tradition.) As for the practitioners of cultural (read ideological) studies, Kermode's judgment of them is severe. He quotes from Julien Benda's famous *La Trahison des Clercs:* "Our age is indeed the age of the intellectual organization of hatred." Kermode remarks, "Benda was of course thinking more of politics than of art, but in our present situation his sentence surely loses nothing of its force. For we all have colleagues who hate or despise literature, and institutional change has given them power."[4]

Kermode has diagnosed a condition. But what to make of his prescription? As an undergraduate at Columbia College in the early 1950s, I remember that literary discussion required a literary sensibility, but was unembarrassed or should I say embarrassed by thoughts of politics and history, though not politics and history in their current tendentious versions. (I'm sure that our New Historicists and cultural materialists would say we had our own tendentious versions, so it may come down to the tendency one prefers.) Is it too late to retrieve cultural studies from the ideologues and perhaps to conceive an alternative version? I hope not, for that would mean conceding an activity as valuable as cultural criticism to the ideology critics. It would also mean an unnecessary contraction of literary study to an internal critique of a work with only occasional reference to history and politics. As a practicing critic, Kermode is among our most historically informed critics with a keen sense of the cultural motives and implications of a work. So I have to think that Kermode's call for a division of labor reflects a despair about the *present* state of cultural studies. If cultural study were still in the hands of Lionel Trilling, Raymond Williams, and Richard Hoggart, I doubt that he would be recommending the insulation of literary studies from it.

The main target of John Ellis's *Literature Lost: Social Agendas and the Corruption of the Humanities* is the preoccupation with "race–gender–class theory" in literary study. His indictment of the literary academy is sweeping, for he finds nothing in the newest criticism to redeem it. Much of what he says are variations on the earlier criticisms of Dinesh D'Souza and Roger Kimball, though his approach to the theoretical assumptions of race–gender–class theory is more analytically rigorous than theirs. Unlike Kimball and D'Souza, Ellis has a theoretical mind.

The novel turn in Ellis's critique is his contention that the radically skeptical assault on Western values is itself an extremist extension of those values. The Enlightenment fostered the critical spirit; now its progeny has without discrimination turned upon the Enlightenment to travesty its achievement. For Ellis the European Enlightenment is the virtually exclusive source of civilized value, undeserving of most of the criticism directed against it: "The spread of Enlightenment values has led to the ending of many . . . un-Enlightened customs, such as cannibalism, human sacrifice, head-hunting—and slavery."[5] There is truth in this statement, but Ellis's failure anywhere in the book to acknowledge the destructive imperial side of Enlightenment ambition arouses suspicion of the ideological partiality of the statement even in an admirer of Enlightenment universalism like myself. Where is Kurtz's "Exterminate all the brutes" in Ellis's understanding of what literature has to teach us about the Enlightenment?

Ellis opposes the Enlightenment to postmodern identity politics. In *Cultivating Humanity: A Classical Defense of Reform in Liberal Education*, Martha Nussbaum also affirms the Enlightenment, but not at the expense of African-American studies, women's studies, or the study of human sexuality. She is careful to distinguish the subjects from the postmodern approach that disparages objectivity and reason. She has the advantage of philosophical training, so she can speak with conviction about the inability of postmodernists to "grapple with the technical issues about physics and language that any modern account of [questions about objectivity and reason] needs to confront." And she makes the sensible suggestion that "philosophy be a large part of the undergraduate curriculum,"[6] if only as an antidote to the sophistry of postmodernism.

Ellis's *Literature Lost* is a political book, more concerned about identity politics than about the literature whose disappearance it laments. He complains that "literary critics are not . . . trained in political analysis, and as we shall see from their attempts at it, they do it badly."[7] For all his complaining, Ellis, himself a literary scholar, writes like a would-be political theorist and rarely addresses literature. And as a political theorist he does not always encourage confidence in his judgment. Consider his rather original definition of political correctness as "a thoroughly Western phenomenon" which he traces back to Tacitus, who "imagined noble Germany as a standard against which to judge the Romans," and more immediately and tellingly Rousseau, who "instead of being content to think that eighteenth-century French society and its institutions were corrupt and corrupting and to imagine another people that was morally superior because their natural goodness had remained intact, generalized [that] man in his natural state was naturally good, and all corruptness sprang from society and its institutions."[8]

According to Ellis, this becomes a model for a cultural relativism which exalts tribal cultures at the expense of Western civilization. Ellis's view of Rousseau's conception of nature and society is reductive and simplistic. More important, however, is his failure to see that Tacitus and Rousseau are examples of a phenomenon that goes back to the Bible— a view of man's fall from an Edenic past into civilization. To characterize the imagination of paradise lost as political correctness is puzzling—and an unwitting irony, given Ellis's conception of literature as lost.

Political correctness does not have a specific content. Quite the contrary, its arbitrariness and coerciveness are in its unpredictability. The party line may change, but it remains correct, whatever it may be. It is correct by virtue of its being the party line. The prototype for political correctness is the behavior of Communist parties during the Stalin period. It may be hyperbolic to compare the behavior of Stalinists with that of the literary academy. But the Stalinist paradigm comes to mind in the conception, most forcefully expressed by Stanley Fish, that it is the interpretive community that authorizes our responses to texts, that we internalize its constraints, and that whatever changes occur within the interpretive community, authority is always with it. Any individual response that defies communal constraints is without interest.

Even more puzzling is Ellis's implied solution to the problem:

In the past, a quality-control mechanism was in place to prevent the corruption and decline of teaching and research: the dean. If deans heard of a classroom where the main focus was not on teaching students how to think and learn but on making them serve—directly serve—political and social ends, they could intervene to insist that classrooms were for education, not for faculty hobbyhorses or social activism.[9]

A dean can intervene where aberrant behavior is concerned, but can hardly be expected to insist that an entire discipline revise its way of doing things. Disciplines have academic freedom to determine their own agendas, no matter how repugnant they may be to a president or a dean. If change is to occur, it must come within the discipline itself.

Not all critics of the current regime are despairing. M. H. Abrams concludes an incisive critique of the alienating effect of the current vogue of suspicious and unmasking readings of a text with a sanguine assertion that literary study will survive in the very transformation that has occurred:

Some fifty years from now the Academy of Arts and Sciences will convene a conference on the transformation of American academic culture, for which a scholar will be commissioned to review the history and condition of English and other literary studies. She will find the analysis and history of literature, both as literature and as inter-involved with other human activities and concerns, to be a prominent component of the academic curriculum. And looking back, she will conclude that literary studies, having undergone some such changes as I have sketched, are (in a favorite expression of my favorite literary theorist, S. T. Coleridge) *alter et idem*. The Latin may be translated freely as "transformed yet recognizable."[10]

Abrams's "prophecy" is surprising, and I must confess unconvincing. It reads more like a wish than a conclusion consistent with his argument. And yet I can sympathize with its spirit, for the alternative is a fruitless all-out culture war of the sort that we have been experiencing in recent years. Such a war benefits neither the academy nor the cultural life in general.

*What's Happened to the Humanities,* edited by Alvin C. Kernan, is a salutary event. If the bias of most of the essays is critical of humanistic studies as practiced in the academy, the contributors prefer to engage in debate or dialogue rather than to conduct war—as in culture wars. Consider the concluding paragraph of Gertrude Himmelfarb's contribution. She believes that a reaction to postmodernism and all its attendant -isms (multiculturalism, New Historicism, radical feminism) may be setting in, but she has no illusion about a return to the status quo ante.

Certainly the new subjects, which now have so much institutional as well as ideological support—African American, ethnic, cultural, multi-cultural, feminist and gender studies—will not disappear. What is not clear is whether these subjects (and the old ones as well) lend themselves to some methodological "middle ground," or what such a methodology might look like. In the meantime, traditionalists and postmodernists alike will have to tolerate and be civil to each other. The real challenge is to do so while understanding the full import of the scholarly revolution that has affected all the humanities.[11]

Himmelfarb has been a severe critic of the cultural left and a formidable polemicist. The polemicist has not disappeared in her essay, but the concluding paragraph represents a change of tone, in effect a call for negotiation. Toleration and civility, of course, will not be enough. One has to think hard about the terms of negotiation.

Critics on the right or center (I dislike employing the language of the Assemblé Nationale to cultural debate, because such language gives a prejudiced and misleading impression about what the issues are) are most effective in their negative criticisms. In his contribution "The Practice of Reading," Denis Donoghue says what has to be said about the current fashion of ideological reductiveness in interpreting literary works. His examples are recent feminist, New Historicist, and psychoanalytic readings of *Macbeth*. Donoghue summarizes his reading of the "new" ideological critics (no longer very new): "[T]he gist of the consensus is that *Macbeth* is Shakespeare's fantasy of male self-begetting and immortality, without recourse to women."[12]

How do these critics arrive at this view? The quotations Donoghue provides give the answer. According to Terry Eagleton:

To any unprejudiced reader—which would seem to exclude Shakespeare himself, his contemporary audience and almost all literary critics—it is surely clear that positive value in *Macbeth* lies with the three witches. The witches are the heroines of the piece, however little the play itself recognizes the fact, and however much the critics may have set out to defame them. It is they who, by releasing ambitious thoughts in Macbeth, expose a reverence for hierarchical social order for what it is, as the pious self-deception of a society based on routine oppression and incessant warfare. The witches are exiles from that violent order, inhabiting their own sisterly community on its shadowy borderlands, refusing all truck with its tribal bickering and military honors.[13]

The witches are heroines after Eagleton's own ideological heart. They not only expose the social order of the play, but deny the play a right to its own understanding. The same is true for passages from other critics Donoghue adduces. The failure of these ideology critics is that they

are queering one discipline—literary criticism—with the habits of another—social science. Their metier is not verbal analysis but the deployment of themes, arguments, and diagnoses: hence the only relation they maintain to the language of *Macbeth* is a remote one. . . . These critics have no sense of the recalcitrance of language, specifically of Shakespeare's English: They think that in reading his words they are engaging with forces and properties indistinguishable from their own.[14]

It is an unremarked irony that the appropriative readings of works of literature by Eagleton and others are supposed to reflect an interest in the historicity of literature, whereas in fact they often show little regard for the actual context and self-understanding of the work itself. They read literature from a political, not an historical perspective. Social science, of course, need not be inimical to the study of literature. It can complement it as sociology of literature. But the distinctions that used to obtain among the sociological, the historical, and the aesthetic disciplines have been lost in current practice. The sociology of literature in its aggressive, demystifying expression has become the dominant form of advanced academic study of literature.

A recent edition of Joyce's *Portrait of the Artist as a Young Man* contains essays illustrating current critical practice: psychoanalytic, feminist, New Historicist, reader-centered. What characterizes most of the essays, whatever the differences among them, is a resistant reading of the work. The reader-centered critic begins by testifying to his lifelong prejudice against the novel, particularly Stephen. He resents Stephen's behavior, Father Arnall's fire and brimstone sermon, the verbal authority of Stephen, and his author as if he were a character in the novel, unhappy that his own interests were not being attended to. The feminist critic is alert to Stephen's misogyny and extrapolates from it his failure as an artist. (How then should we account for Strindberg's success?) The New Historicist remarks Joyce's racialist view of genius (persuasively providing an historical context) and, from a Foucauldian perspective, the futility of the individual's revolt (genius or not) against institutional authority.

Stephen is something of an egomaniac and a misogynist; the priest's sermon does not reflect well on his religion; and Joyce may have shared the racialist conception of his contemporaries. However, the failure in these approaches is in the hardly qualified resistance to the novels. In their unwillingness or inability to sympathize with Stephen they cannot participate in the double movement of the narrative voice in the novel; the movement of sympathy and irony. Stephen's intellectual and imaginative power is unmistakable, and it should not be hard to see that for him Art may be the only alternative to the fraught world of Dublin, to which its political and religious squalor and violence Stephen is a terror-stricken witness. Joyce affirms and criticizes Stephen's ambition. Stephen himself mocks his own extravagant revolutionary gestures ("the spiritual-heroic refrigerating apparatus, invented and patented in all countries by Dante Alighieri") at the same time that he grandiosely asserts his Shel-leyan ambition to create the conscience of his race. Joyce's ambivalence toward Stephen (Stephen's ambivalence toward himself) is a model for the critical reader. Without the possibility of sympathetic identification with Stephen, why would the reader take an interest in the novel—ex-cept perhaps as a case in cultural pathology? The problem extends be-yond the politicizing of literature to the deliberate appropriation of works to a variety of interests without significant regard to the interests of the works themselves.

Still another example: Hardy's *Tess of the d'Urbervilles* arouses strong feeling whenever the discussion turns to the question of whether Tess was raped or seduced by Alec d'Urberville. The question is not raised in the novel, so why even introduce the terms and raise the ques-tion? Seduction suggests arousal—arousal even against one's own will, rape, sheer violence, and coercion. There is evidence throughout the novel that Tess was aroused by Alec against her will. She was "dazzled" by his manners. She is characterized as having an "incautious nature," of being "deep-passioned." The actual representation of the event is veiled as we would expect from a Victorian writer; the passage gives the impression of pastoral sadness, but no violence. What is at stake for the feminist-inspired claim that Tess was raped is a redefinition of rape, which extends its meaning to cover, for example, seduction in the face of conscious resistance. The issue is not the validity of such a redefini-tion in our time, but whether it applies to an understanding of the novel. Our contemporary understandings should not become a screen that prevents us from understanding the novel in its own terms, specifically from seeing Tess as Hardy created her.

My examples are from the cultural left, but the phenomenon is not confined to the left. If the discourses of race, ethnicity, gender, and class have their source in the cultural left, they have nevertheless become the common property of educated people inside and outside the academy, regardless of political persuasion. For example, T. S. Eliot's anti-Semitism has been the subject of study by Antony Julius, a lawyer by profession, a classical liberal, but not an example of the cultural left. It is doubtful, however, whether his attention would have turned to his subject if it weren't for the current preoccupation with identity politics and ethnicity. His book is an antidote (necessary, but excessive in the dosage Julius administers) to the complacent responses to anti-Semitism such as those of William Empson or George Orwell, who characterized the anti-Semitism they heard around them as "garden variety." "Who didn't say such things at the time?" Orwell remarked. Julius effectively counters by exposing the virulence of lines such as "And the jew squats on the window sill, the owner, / spawned in some estaminet of Antwerp, / Blistered in Brussels, patched and peeled in London" ("Gerontion") and "The rats are underneath the piles / the jew is under the lot / Money in furs" ("Burbank with a Baedeker; Bleustein with a Cigar") and its affinities with the most vicious of anti-Semitic passages of Charles Maurras, of the notorious Action Française, Edouard-Adolphe Drumont, and of Bram Dijkstra. Unfortunately, the preoccupation with anti-Semitism consumes Julius's view of Eliot. The persuaded reader should come away from the book believing not simply that anti-Semitism infects Eliot's work, but that it is his muse. Critical balance is lost in an effort to indict the poet.[15]

To return to Donoghue: He focuses on language, but what he says applies as well to the ideas and themes of the work. He concludes on a muted hopeful note: "I have been heartened recently, reading certain critics who might be thought to be entirely 'political' and finding them coming around again to the recognition of aesthetics as a necessary discipline of attention."[16] Perhaps the barricades are beginning to come down, Donoghue seems to be saying, and common ground is possible.

I am in sympathy with Donoghue's view as far as it goes. The critics of the politicization of literary study need now to come forward with ideas about the role of politics and ideology in literary understanding. What to do, for instance, with the ideological aspect of a work? It cannot be ignored, if the middle ground Himmelfarb hopes for is to be found. The relationship between the aesthetic and the ideological is not addressed in Kernan's collection, though it invites attention.

There is, of course, a tension, if not outright conflict, between aesthetics and ideology. Aesthetics, inspired by the work of the third Earl of Shaftesbury, has generally stood for the autonomy of the work of art, the disinterested contemplation of beauty; ideology denies disinterestedness and autonomy, defining, as it does, the conditions of which the creative mind is hardly aware, conditions that determine its productions. So an interest in both aesthetics and ideology requires doublemindedness. Is such doublemindedness possible to a critical reader, or is it as impossible a task as traveling simultaneously in opposite directions?

The problem is alleviated if one gives up the radical Marxist version of ideology as false consciousness, the version that Eagleton represents in his comment about *Macbeth* and elsewhere. In such a version, the text never knows itself, all the wisdom is in the demystifying modern reader. (I have criticized this view in my recent book, *The Reign of Ideology.*) On the opposite side of the spectrum is an impoverishing aestheticism which effectively denies the ideological or philosophical aspect of a work of literature—denies it by absorbing into a triumphant aesthetic form. It is not the case that the greatest literature eschews ideology. Dostoevsky's novels contain characters possessed by ideology. Kirilov and Stavrogin in *The Possessed* are ideologues, knowingly exposed in the narrative (without the benefit of an Eagleton), and Dostoevsky himself is a profound ideological writer (with an ideology), as Joseph Frank has shown in his magisterial critical biography. But it becomes a question in considering any particular work whether the aesthetic achievement contains the ideology or whether it is determined by it—put differently, whether the ideological conditions of its making determine the character of a work or whether they remain conditions that can be transcended.

This may be a moment in the history of literary study to affirm the rhetorical (in the older sense) and the aesthetic against excessively polarized interpretations of literature, and especially interpretation politicized on one end of the political spectrum. But it may also be the moment for critics of the profession to begin thinking *freshly* about ideology, history, and politics in literary study. Critics of the profession have for too long had a parasitic relation to the present state of affairs, exposing absurdities, not giving credit where credit was due, and, most important of all, providing little in the way of a positive perspective.

In *The Rules of Art,* the sociologist Pierre Bourdieu has thought freshly on these matters. I must confess to surprise, because his work, whenever I have tried to engage it in the past, has impressed me as reader-unfriendly. It has seemed to me full of jargon and tendentious. Nevertheless, *The Rules of Art* is a real achievement. Bourdieu's text is Flaubert and the idea of the autonomy of art. His aim is to specify the historical conditions of the emergence of the idea without demystifying it. Sociology becomes in Bourdieu's hands a species of literary criticism, as in his discussion of *Sentimental Education:*

One feels Flaubert is wholly there, in the universe of relationships that would have to be explored one by one, in their double dimension, both artistic and social, and that he nevertheless remains irreducibly beyond it: is this not because the active integration that he effects implies an overcoming? In situating himself, as it were, at the geometric intersection of all perspectives, which is also the point of greatest tension, he forces himself in some fashion to raise to their highest intensity the set of questions in the field, to play out all the resources inscribed in the space of possibilities that, in the manner of a language or musical instrument, is offered each writer, like an infinite universe of possible combinations locked in a potential state within the finite system of constraints.[17]

This is not perspicuous prose (the last sentence is particularly unfortunate), but it deserves a generous translation. Bourdieu captures what most ideology critics fail or refuse to see: the artist's capacity to represent the conflicting interests of his characters in a fiction with an intensity that paradoxically does not commit him to one side or another. He is "at the geometric intersection of all perspectives" at "the point of greatest tension." Here is a glimpse of what the autonomy of art means— or what it doesn't mean. It doesn't mean the irrelevance of nonaesthetic considerations like history and politics nor of the conditions of production. It does mean that there is a dimension in a work that cannot simply be reduced to these conditions and that may indeed embody and master them. The artist has the capacity to be both inside and outside his world.

In response to the complaint that the sociology of literature has the effect of "'leveling' artistic values by 'rehabilitating' second-rate authors," Bourdieu argues persuasively that one can understand the individuality and greatness of the authors who have survived by studying "the universe of contemporaries with whom and against whom they constructed themselves." And he shows how Flaubert emerges as the distinctive figure that he is in the French literary tradition "through the whole series of double negations with which he counters contrasting pairs of styles or authors—like Romanticism and realism, Lamartine and Champfeury, and so forth."[18] Bourdieu's approach contrasts with a sociological view, pervasive in literary studies, that ignores artistic distinction in the interest of the documentary value of a work, and with an ideological approach that regards the aesthetic aspect as the mystification of motives of domination.

Those defending current practice can point to the past and note that politics has always been present in literary study. "What you object to is not our politicizing of literature, but the particular content of our politics," I can imagine a defender saying. There is a conservative view that complains about multiculturalism and identity politics in and out of literary studies, but it has its own politics: the fostering of good citizenship and the cultivation of virtue. So there is appropriation on both sides of the spectrum.

There has always been a place for political criticism of literature, or I should say a criticism of politics in a literary work. In recent times the New York intellectuals rarely kept political and extraliterary historical concerns out of their literary criticism. And even the New Critics, often invoked for their purely formalist ideal (a distorted view of their practice), reflected on the evils of modernity from a conservative point of view. I recall reading a book on the reactionary character of the writers of high modernism, John Harrison's *The Reactionaries,* in the 1960s before the current practice of ideology critique. I thought the book insufficiently responsive to the literary character of the works discussed, but it did have the virtue (not common to critical practice at the time) of alertness to the distressing association of our most gifted writers with the most reactionary tendencies of the time, including fascism. Here is an ambiguity. The writing of literature should be an insubordinate activity; it should not have to submit to a political or moral litmus test of any kind. And yet a work of literature may offend political and moral sensibilities, and a critic may declare his revulsion from a work. The critic then may pass political and moral judgment, but only after he has made an effort to understand a work in its own terms.

If a middle ground is to be achieved, the critics of the discipline must acknowledge its achievements, and its practitioners must take to heart the criticisms. Recent scholarship has been responsible for the recovery of neglected worthwhile writing by women, African Americans, and writers of other ethnic backgrounds. And even where the writing has been second-rate and worse, it may have historical interest or provide that "universe of contemporaries with whom and against whom [major writers] have constructed themselves," as Bourdieu puts it. (It remains for the discipline, however, to follow such a program. To do so, it will have to become once more interested in artistic distinction.) The concern with gender, for example, has created an awareness of the repressive way the marriage plot sometimes functions in the nineteenth-century novel. The eponymous heroine of Jane Austen's *Emma* says it is not in her nature to marry, only to find herself having to satisfy the requirements of the marriage plot. It is at least an open question of whether Emma is deceived about where her true interest lies when she declares herself not to be the marrying kind or whether the plot acts coercively against Emma's nature. (This open question, raised in connection with other novels, however, is often answered by doctrinaire assertions about the tyranny of the marriage plot and the institution it affirms.) Then there is the imperial theme, the focus of postcolonial studies. I recall my first encounter with *Heart of Darkness* in the 1950s in which little matters apart from Marlow's psychological drama on his African journey; the Freudian triad of ego–superego–id was all the rage. It is salutary to be reminded that Marlow and other characters in the tale are agents of empire. (It is depressing, however, to be required to read every work in which empire is a theme, major or minor, as a story of imperial oppression.)

The concern with race–gender–class and postcolonialism may persist, but it must surrender its virtual monopoly in the field. Critical practice, whatever its object, must recover literary sensibility—and "tact," a word used in the past to describe the delicate and complex engagement of a work by critical readers. The middle ground would accept not only the new subject matter, but the questions they provoke, for example, those that I gave as examples of questions that figure in current academic discussion. Colonialism in Shakespeare? Complicity with patriarchy in Jane Austen? Imperialism and racism in Conrad? The significance of anti-Semitism in Eliot? Such questions do *not* get raised in aesthetic criticism. But these are questions that a scholar or critic would *not* be required to raise as a matter of course. It is still possible to provide an interesting and persuasive reading of Shakespeare, Austen, Conrad, and Eliot without pressing these questions on them. Nor should the answers to the questions when addressed be constricted by an ideological agenda. For example, the answer to the question of whether Jane Austen is complicit with patriarchy in the celebration of the marriage of her heroines is not simply yes or no. We need to understand what is meant by the words "complicity" and "patriarchy" as it applies to Austen's novels. Marriage is an institution so rich in tradition, social meaning, and personal affect that it cannot simply be reduced to masculine authority and abuse. Always fraught with risks of misunderstanding and oppression, marriage in an Austen novel nevertheless appeals to us in its *promesse de bonheur.*

Or consider the study of ethnicity and race. It need not be the captive of identity politics. One may, for instance, approach the question of ethnic or racial identity in terms of its contribution to the cosmopolitan spirit of the literary imagination. In a fine recent study of Oscar Wilde, Julia Prewitt Brown speaks of "the ethnic element as essential to any authentic cosmopolitanism: it is the basis of the cosmopolitan's curious, melancholy, voluntary exile,"[19] by which I suppose she means that every artist who aims to transcend his ethnic origins never escapes his residual attachment to them—an attachment, for instance, that expresses itself in Joyce's love–hate relationship to Ireland. Joyce is a particularly fruitful opportunity for the study of the ethnic element. In *Portrait of the Artist as a Young Man,* Stephen, Joyce's stand-in, believed that he could escape the nets of Church, nation, and family (his Irishness) by entering the realm of art. We are all familiar with Stephen's triumphant declaration that the artist can create the conscience of his race. But in *Ulysses* Stephen proves to be a failure, and we must wonder what in his commitment to art contributed to it. Art in its exalted version is an abstraction, insufficiently rooted in the particularity of living. And Joyce knew this all too well when he created Leopold Bloom, a nonreligious Jew with Enlightenment affinities. Bloom is a paradox: a character whose universality is rooted in his Jewishness ("their eyes knew the years of wandering and, patient, knew the dishonours of the flesh"[20]) and whose rootlessness makes him the ubiquitous and acute observer of the Dublin scene. In creating Leopold Bloom, Joyce freed himself from his identification with the aesthetical Stephen and found a route back to the common life. The Enlightenment Jew may have certain advantages over other ethnics in representing cosmopolitan or universalist aspirations, but every ethnicity has in it an aspiration to represent something larger than itself. Joyce draws parallels among the Jew, the Irishman, and the Greek, all subject to the oppressions of empire (Egyptian, English, and Roman) and all bearers of a cultural idea larger than their ethnicities.

Isn't this the claim that Ralph Ellison makes for black experience, when he resists the criticism of those who want to know why Hemingway was more important to him than Richard Wright, in effect refusing to be ghettoized as a Negro writer and yet at the same time finding in his black experience the very spirit of tragedy and America? "Because all he [Hemingway] wrote—and this is very important—was imbued with a spirit beyond the tragic with which I could feel at home, for it was very close to the feeling of the blues, which are, perhaps, as close as Americans can come to expressing the spirit of tragedy."[21]

History, society, politics: They are the inevitable part of literary discussion. Under a new dispensation, they would include perspectives on the whole political and moral spectrum. The middle ground would also allow a space for an apolitical aesthetic interest in literature.

The new subject matter should benefit from the exercise of an aesthetic discipline that discriminates between works that achieve the condition of art and those that have at best a documentary value. It does not represent progress to conflate literary criticism with an historicism that is really a sociology of literature animated by ideological motives. We need to relearn the value of distinguishing between Ellison's *Invisible Man* and Alice Walker's *The Color Purple*, between Henry Roth's *Call It Sleep* and Abraham Cahan's *The Rise of David Levinsky*, between Henry James's *A Portrait of a Lady* and Theodore Dreiser's *An American Tragedy*. Is this elitism? Like domination and hegemony, the word has been charged with pejorative meaning, the effect of which is to prevent us from seeing what would be lost, if the faculty of *literary* discrimination disappeared.

The Jeremiahs of the profession may be proven right that literary study will become an esoteric subject, giving way to communications and media study. It may also be the case that renewed interest in aesthetics combined with a more generous conception of historical context and political content will revive the study of literature. What is not clear is how this will be accomplished. The future of the profession belongs to the current crop of graduate students or those among them fortunate enough to get jobs. How in practice does one create the middle ground, if graduate education in literary study is preoccupied with race, ethnic, and postcolonial discourse? Where will we find the cohort of the next generation of scholars willing and able to work outside the prevailing preoccupations? A political stance against these preoccupations must give way to dialogue. Eleanor Cook, the president of the newly formed Association of Literary Scholars and Critics (ALSC), devoted to "broad conceptions of literature, rather than the highly politicized ones encountered today," writes in a newsletter of the organization of the need of students to acquire "a precise knowledge of the workings of literature, and skill in using it. An older terminology would say that we teach rhetoric . . . disinterested or Aristotelian rhetoric: a mapping of tropes, schemes, and so on, and the ways they work." A knowledge of literary form is indispensable and prior to "any interest in questions raised by deconstruction, feminist readings, new historicism and so on."[22] Cook may not be speaking for everyone in the organization, but her presidential statement suggests that the ALSC does not want to exacerbate the polarization of the field. Indeed, she writes in an irenic spirit, suggesting the possibility of a reconciliation between a disinterested formalist approach and the newer interested ideological uses of literature. One should begin with a precise knowledge of the workings of literature and follow with whatever appropriation one wishes to make of it. Presumably, the requirement of precise knowledge would provide an obstacle to some of the cruder exercises in ideological criticism. I can imagine objections to this view from opposite sides. The deconstructionist, feminist, and New Historicist see themselves in competition with the formalists in their understanding of how literature works; those opposed to deconstructionism, feminism, and New Historicism would agree that they are competitive and assert that they distort literary works. It may not be clear at the present time how Cook's conciliatory proposal can be realized. But it is at least a call for the kind of dialogue that the discipline sorely needs.

In a recent newsletter of the ALSC (Fall 1998), there is a report of a debate between "some members [who] thought that it was time for militant statements of principle in opposition to organizations that have 'bastardized language and thought' and 'a larger contingent [that] argued against the Association being diverted from its example-setting focus on literature.'" A focus on literature does not preclude polemics. I have tried in my own writing to balance the polemical with an attention to the work of literature and indeed polemics may often be a way into an understanding of literary work. Do we need, however, *"militant* statements of principle" (emphasis added). Militancy is what the ideological critics have given us. What we need now, I think, is a polemics which cannot always be distinguished from dialogue. Since the future of the profession belongs to our graduate students, scholars unhappy with the state of the profession will have to accommodate what the students have already learned, for instance, matters of race, gender, and class. By accommodation I mean dialogue, not capitulation. Unless we (and I include myself among those unhappy with the profession) display a willingness to listen and respond to what may be a value in the current way of doing things, and unless we address the problem of employment and status in the profession (i.e., the dissatisfaction of young Ph.D.s who become part-time instructors without a franchise in the profession), we will lose whatever chance we have to be listened to. Militancy has been the bane of the profession, the very antithesis to the disinterested pursuit of knowledge, which has been the ideal of the profession for over a hundred years.

There is reason for pessimism. But there is also reason for hope. So long as there are teachers and students with at least a residual affection for literature, it is possible that there will be a return (but always with a difference) to the literary study of literature. I have no prophecies to make, but without hope there would be little point in writing this book.

Notes

Index

# Notes

## Preface

1. John Henry Newman, "Knowledge Its Own End," in *The Idea of a University* (1852).
2. Henry Adams, *The Education of Henry Adams* (1905; New York: Modern Library, 1931), 192.

## Chapter 1

1. Gerald Graff and Michael Warner, *The Origins of Literary Study in America* (New York: Routledge, 1989), 8.
2. Ibid., 13.
3. Gerald Graff, "Preaching to the Converted," in Susan Gubar and Joan Kamholtz, eds., *English Inside and Out: The Places of Literary Criticism* (New York and London: Routledge, 1993), 118.
4. Ibid., 120.
5. Graff, *Beyond the Culture Wars* (New York: Norton, 1992), 52.
6. John Stuart Mill, "Bentham," in Gertrude Himmelfarb, ed., *Essays on Politics and Culture* (Gloucester, Mass.: Peter Smith, 1973), 92.
7. Graff, *Beyond the Culture Wars,* 7.
8. Graff and Warner, *Origins of Literary Study,* 11–12.
9. David Damrosch, "A Past We Can Live With," *Civilization* (April–May, 1997): 77.
10. Alan Wolfe, *Marginalized in the Middle* (Chicago: Univ. of Chicago Press, 1996), 34.
11. David Bromwich, *Politics by Other Means: Higher Education and Group Thinking* (New Haven: Yale Univ. Press, 1992), 106.
12. Peter Brooks, "What Happened to Poetics," in George Levine, ed., *Aesthetics and Ideology,* (New Brunswick: Rutgers Univ. Press, 1994), 11.

123

13. Harold Bloom, *The Western Canon: The Books and School of the Ages* (New York: Harcourt, Brace, 1994), 8–9.

14. Tzvetan Todorov, "Crimes Against Humanities," *The New Republic* (July 3, 1989): 30.

15. See Allan Bloom, *The Closing of the American Mind* (New York: Simon and Schuster, 1987).

16. See Martha Nussbaum, *Cultivating Humanity: A Classical Defense of Reform in Liberal Education* (Cambridge: Harvard Univ. Press, 1997).

17. See Stephen Holmes, *The Anatomy of Antiliberalism* (Cambridge: Harvard Univ. Press, 1993), 14.

18. Levine, ed., *Aesthetics and Ideology*, 11.

19. See Todd Gitlin, *The Twilight of Common Dreams: Why America Is Wracked by Culture Wars* (New York: Metropolitan Books, Henry Holt, 1995).

20. Peter Novick, *That Noble Dream: The "Objectivity Question" and the American Historical Profession* (New York: Cambridge Univ. Press, 1988), 523.

21. See ibid., 596.

22. See Alan B. Spitzer, *Historical Truth and Lies about the Past* (Chapel Hill: Univ. of North Carolina Press, 1996).

23. Novick, *That Noble Dream*, 12, 14.

24. Richard Rorty, "Does Academic Freedom Have Philosophical Presuppositions," in Louis Menand, ed., *The Future of Academic Freedom* (Chicago: Univ. of Chicago Press, 1996), 21.

25. Ibid., 27.

26. Evelyn Fox Keller, "Science and Its Critics," in ibid., 211.

27. See Denis Donoghue, "The Joy of Texts," review of Robert Alter's *The Pleasures of Reading in an Ideological Age, The New Republic* 200, no. 6 (June 26, 1989): 17.

28. *Lingua Franca* (July/Aug. 1996): 60.

29. Lynn Hunt, "Democratization and Decline? The Consequences of Democratic Change in the Humanities," in Alvin Kernan, ed., *What's Happened to the Humanities* (Princeton: Princeton Univ. Press, 1996), 17.

30. Francis Oakley, "Ignorant Armies and Nighttime Clashes: Changes in the Humanities Classroom 1970–95," in ibid., 67.

31. Eugene Goodheart, *The Reign of Ideology* (New York: Columbia Univ. Press, 1996), 19.

32. Jane Gallop, "The Institutionalization of Feminist Criticism," in Gubar and Kamholtz, eds., *English Inside and Out*, 65.

33. Gerald Graff, *Professing Literature: An Institutional History* (Chicago: Univ. of Chicago Press, 1987), 123–24.

34. Levine, ed., *Aesthetics and Ideology*, 11.

35. Ibid., 11.

36. Ibid., 14.

37. Keller, "Science and Its Critics," 204.

38. Brooks, "What Happened to Poetics," 158.

39. Jerome Stolnitz, *Aesthetics and the Philosophy of Art Criticism* (Boston: Houghton Mifflin, 1960), 34–35.

40. Linda Dowling, *The Vulgarization of Art: The Victorians and Aesthetic Democracy* (Charlottesville and London: Univ. of Virginia Press, 1996), 4.

41. Ibid., 13.

42. Ibid., 10.

43. Ibid., 61.

44. Bloom, *Western Canon*, 33.

45. See Ronald Paulson, *The Beautiful, Novel, and Strange: Aesthetics and Heterodoxy* (Baltimore: Johns Hopkins Univ. Press, 1996).

46. Robert Hughes, *The Culture of Complaint: The Fraying of America* (New York: Oxford Univ. Press, 1993), 79.

47. See Morris Dickstein, "Journalism as Criticism," in *Double Agent: The Critic and Society* (New York: Oxford Univ. Press, 1992), 55–67.

48. Bloom, *Western Canon*, 18.

## Chapter 2

1. Alan Wolfe, *Marginalized in the Middle* (Chicago: Univ. of Chicago Press, 1996), 91.

2. Homi Bhabba, "Of Mimicry and Man: The Ambivalence of Colonialist Discourse," in Annette Michelson, ed., *October: The First Decade: 1976–86* (Cambridge: MIT Press, 1986), 318, 324–25. Quoted in Roger Kimball, *Tenured Radicals* (New York: Harper and Row, 1990), 93.

3. Nancy Chodorow, "Toward a Relational Individualism: The Mediation of the Self Through Psychoanalysis," in Thomas Heller, Morton Sosna, and David Wellbery, eds., *Reconstructing Individualism*, (Stanford: Stanford University Press, 1986), 197. Quoted in Kimball, *Tenured Radicals*, 47.

4. Kimball, *Tenured Radicals*, 47–48.

5. Chodorow, "Toward a Relational Individualism," 198.

6. Kimball, *Tenured Radicals*, 105.

7. Ibid., 59.

8. Ibid., 138.

9. Matthew Arnold, *Culture and Anarchy,* edited by Samuel Lipman (1869; New Haven: Yale Univ. Press, 1994), 71.

10. Ibid., 135.

11. "The Function of Criticism at the Present Time," in Matthew Arnold, *Selected Essays,* edited by Noel Annan (London: Oxford Univ. Press, 1964), 31.

12. Samuel Lipman, "Why Should We Read *Culture and Anarchy?,*" in Arnold, *Culture and Anarchy,* 225.

13. Ibid., 218.

14. Arnold, *Selected Essays,* 39.

15. Dinesh D'Souza, *Illiberal Education: The Politics of Race and Sex on Campus* (New York: Free Press), 13.

16. Ibid., 14.

17. Rene Wellek and Austin Warren, *Theory of Literature* (New York: Harcourt, Brace, 1949), 32.

18. Ibid., 175.

19. Ibid., 255–56.

## Chapter 3

1. Gary Wills, *The New York Times Magazine,* Feb. 16, 1997, section B, 42.

2. Ibid.

3. Bernard Bergonzi, *Exploding English: Criticism, Theory, Culture* (Oxford: Clarendon Press, 1990), 118. Bergonzi is paraphrasing Michael Ryan.

4. Harold Bloom, *The Western Canon: The Books and School of the Ages:* (New York: Harcourt and Brace, 1994), 3.

5. Hillis Miller, *Theory Now and Then* (Durham: Duke Univ. Press, 1991), 391.

6. See Denis Donoghue, "The Practice of Reading," in Alvin Kernan, ed., *What's Happened to the Humanities?* (Princeton: Princeton Univ. Press, 1997), 135.

7. Frank Kermode, *The Classic: Literary Images of Permanence and Change* (New York: Viking, 1975), 15. All subsequent references are in the body of the text.

8. Barbara Herrnstein Smith, "Contingencies of Value," *Critical Inquiry* (September 1983), 31.

9. Ibid., 10.

10. Bloom, *Western Canon,* 30.

11. David Denby, *Great Books: My Adventures with Homer, Rousseau,*

*Woolf and Other Indestructible Writers of the Western World* (New York: Simon and Schuster, 1996), 12. All subsequent references are in the body of the text.

12. Robert Scholes, *Textual Power* (New Haven: Yale Univ. Press, 1985), 23–24.

13. Ibid., 154.

14. Ibid., 24.

15. Louis Menand, "Culture and Advocacy," in Patricia Meyer Spacks, ed., *Advocacy in the Classroom: Problems and Possibilities* (New York: St. Martin's Press, 1996), 117.

16. Helen Vendler, "The Booby Trap," *The New Republic* (Oct. 7, 1996): 37.

17. Lionel Trilling, *Beyond Culture* (New York: Viking, 1955), 27.

18. Gerald Graff, *Professing Literature: An Institutional History* (Chicago: Univ. of Chicago Press, 1987), 252.

19. See Eve Sedgwick, "The Beast in the Closet," in *Epistemology of the Closet* (Berkeley: Univ. of California Press, 1990), 182–212.

20. Graff, *Professing Literature*, 248.

21. Charles Dickens, *Great Expectations*, ed. Janice Carlisle (1861; New York: Bedford Books of St. Martin's Press, 1996), 457. All subsequent references are in the body of the text.

22. David Bromwich, *Politics by Other Means: Higher Education and Group Thinking* (New Haven: Yale Univ. Press, 1992), 196.

23. Quoted in Bergonzi, *Exploding English*, 95.

24. Graff, *Beyond the Culture Wars*, (New York: Norton, 1992), 64.

25. Ibid., 67.

26. Roland Barthes, *S/Z* (New York: Hill & Wang, 1974), 67.

27. Ibid., 156.

28. Ibid., ix.

29. Ibid., xi.

30. Ford Madox Ford, *The Good Soldier* (1927; New York: Vintage, 1983), 55.

31. Philip Roth, *The Counterlife* (New York: Farrar, Strauss & Giroux, 1987), 319–21.

32. Philip Roth, *American Pastoral* (Boston: Houghton Mifflin, 1997), 329.


## Chapter 4

1. Don DeLillo, *White Noise* (New York: Viking, 1986), 50.

2. Ibid., 51.

3. Ibid., 284–85.

4. Ibid., 285.

5. Ibid., 218–19.

6. Andrew Ross, *No Respect* (New York: Oxford Univ. Press, 1989), 3.

7. Ibid., 5.

8. Ibid., 35.

9. Ibid., 144-45.

10. Ibid., 149.

11. Ibid., 151.

12. Andy Warhol, *The Philosophy of Andy Warhol: From A to B and Back Again* (New York: Harcourt Brace Jovanovich, 1975), 93. Quoted in Ross, *No Respect*, 170.

13. Warhol, *The Philosophy of Andy Warhol*, 170.

14. Ibid., 210.

15. Ibid., 211.

16. Ibid., 198.

17. Quoted in Martha Woodmansee, *The Author, Art and the Market: Rereading the History of Aesthetics* (New York: Columbia Univ. Press, 1994), 135.

18. Ibid., 136.

19. Ibid., 142.

20. Millicent Bell, *Meaning in Henry James* (Cambridge: Harvard Univ. Press, 1991), 21.

21. Ibid., 333.

22. Ibid., 300.

23. Ian Bell, *Henry James and the Past* (New York: St. Martin's Press, 1991), 33.

24. Ibid., 55.

25. Ibid., 292.

26. Ibid., 64.

27. Ibid., 13.

28. James Engell and Anthony Dangerfield, "Humanities in the Age of Money," *Harvard Magazine* (May–June 1998): 52.


## Chapter 5

1. See Robert Scholes, *The Rise and Fall of English: Reconstructing English as a Discipline* (New Haven: Yale Univ. Press, 1998)

2. Harold Bloom, *The Western Canon: The Books and School of the Ages* (New York: Harcourt and Brace, 1994).

3. Frank Kermode, "Changing Epochs," in Alvin Kernan, ed., *What's Happened to the Humanities* (Princeton: Princeton Univ. Press, 1997), 176. See also Bernard Bergonzi, *Exploding English: Criticism, Theory, Culture* (Oxford: Clarendon, 1990), 100–101.

4. Kermode, "Changing Epochs," 177.

5. John Ellis, *Literature Lost: Social Agendas and the Corruption of the Humanities* (New Haven: Yale Univ. Press, 1997), 94.

6. Martha Nussbaum, *Cultivating Humanity: A Classical Defense of Reform in Liberal Education* (Cambridge: Harvard Univ. Press, 1997), 40–41.

7. Ellis, *Literature Lost*, 65.

8. Ibid., 15.

9. Ibid., 230.

10. M. H. Abrams, "The Transformation of English Studies: 1930–1995," *Daedalus* (Winter 1997): 129.

11. Gertrude Himmelfarb, "Beyond Method," in Kernan, ed., *What's Happened to the Humanities*, 156–57.

12. Denis Donoghue, "The Practice of Reading," in ibid., 130.

13. Quoted in ibid. Terry Eagleton, *William Shakespeare* (Oxford: Basil Blackwell, 1986), 1–2.

14. Donoghue, "The Practice of Reading," 131.

15. See Antony Julius, *T. S. Eliot and Literary Form* (Cambridge: Cambridge Univ. Press, 1995).

16. Donoghue, "The Practice of Reading," 138.

17. Pierre Bourdieu, *The Rules of Art: Genesis and Structure of the Literary Field* (Stanford: Stanford Univ. Press, 1992), 100.

18. Ibid., 70–71.

19. Julia Prewitt Brown, *Cosmopolitan Criticism: Oscar Wilde's Philosophy of Art* (Charlottesville: Univ. of Virginia Press, 1997) 24.

20. James Joyce, *Ulysses* (New York: Vintage Books), 63.

21. Ralph Ellison, *Shadow and Act* (New York: New American Library, 1953–87), 140.

22. Eleanor Cook, ALSC Newsletter (Spring 1998), 2.

# Index

131